ONE HUNDRED AND THREE FIGHTS
AND SCRIMMAGES

Captain Reuben F. Bernard, 1st Cavalry
Photographed at Walla Walla, Washington, probably in 1878.

One Hundred and Three Fights and Scrimmages

The Story of
GENERAL REUBEN F. BERNARD

By Don Russell

Illustrated by Donald L. Dickson

Reprinted from The Cavalry Journal

WASHINGTON, D. C.
UNITED STATES CAVALRY ASSOCIATION
1936

PRINTED IN THE UNITED STATES BY
GARRETT & MASSIE, RICHMOND, VIRGINIA

CONTENTS

ILLUSTRATIONS AND MAPS

ONE HUNDRED AND THREE FIGHTS AND SCRIMMAGES

BIBLIOGRAPHICAL NOTE: The principal sources are General Bernard's official reports, correspondence, general and special orders, diaries, journals and extracts from muster rolls that have been collected by Brigadier General W. C. Brown, Retired. Bernard's personal record at Headquarters, First U. S. Cavalry (Mecz.), Fort Knox, Kentucky, is very complete. His record at the office of the Order of Indian Wars of the United States, in Washington, D. C., and in *Powell's Records of Living Officers of the United States Army* (Philadelphia, 1890), contains the list of 103 fights. Valuable reminiscences have been contributed by Colonel W. C. Babcock, Retired, and Mrs. Babcock, Brigadier General B. B. Buck, Retired, Mrs. J. T. Crabbs, and Major Charles B. Hardin, Retired.

I

A TENNESSEE D'ARTAGNAN*

WHEN the immortal d'Artagnan makes his first appearance in the pages of Dumas he is described as possessing a yellow pony, thirteen years old, with no hair on its tail, but not without windgalls on its legs, a long rapier that struck against the calves of its owner when he was on foot and the shaggy coat of his steed when he was on horseback, and a letter to the commandant of the King's Musketeers. This equipment, unromantic as it appears in the early pages of that masterpiece of adventure, was princely compared to that possessed by Reuben Frank Bernard, hero of one hundred and three "fights and scrimmages," as he boasted, in the United States dragoons.

For Reuben Bernard was driven into a career of derring do by the single, unromantic possession of a bad case of hay fever.

It is entirely improbable that you have ever heard of Reuben Bernard. No more would you have heard of d'Artagnan had not that adventurer left some very dull and uninspiring volumes of memoirs which the genius of Dumas converted into a superb story. Unfortunately Bernard left not even memoirs—only a few scattered diaries and letters, scant mention in books of his period, and dull and uninspiring official records of an amazing career. Sadly, there is no Dumas to make of these the story that could and should be written. But, just as there really was a d'Artagnan in a company of the King's Musketeers who had amazing adventures, so there was a

*The description of Bernard's leaving home and subsequent details is based largely on material supplied by General B. B. Buck. Imagination has added little to his vivid account.

Reuben Bernard in the First Regiment of United States Dragoons whose story is worth the telling, however unworthily the task may be performed.

Our story begins in that Gascony of the United States, the mountain region of eastern Tennessee. Here we find a country boy, in the years before the Civil War, engaged in hoeing corn. In that one sentence you may immediately establish his social status, and dismiss from your minds any notion of blue-blooded Southern aristocracy. In case you have forgotten, it was from this region that came those staunch Unionists Andrew Jackson and Andrew Johnson, and so largely did its people adhere to the federal cause in the Civil War that several rather useless military campaigns were waged with the object of bringing them within the Union lines.

But it was not patriotism that brought Reuben Bernard to embrace a military career. It was, as I have said, hay fever.

No modern allergic tests were necessary to determine the cause of this trouble. He knew, as well as medical science could now have told him, that every time his hoe struck a corn tassel, knocking loose a fine spray of yellow pollen, he took to coughing and sneezing. It was a very hot day. The corn tassels were very ripe. Perhaps he had other troubles. We know that he was one of fourteen brothers and sisters, of whom two are known to have died in infancy. It might be interesting to note here that three of his brothers were killed in action during the Civil War, a point that gives some hint as to the quality of the family. But it may well be imagined that John Bernard, Sr., and Mary Morelock Bernard, his wife, found it a problem beyond their solution to wrest a living from the scant soil of Hawkins County, Tennessee, for their ever growing family. At this period, although the eldest daughter,

Annie, was 25, and the eldest son, Reuben, was nearly 22, the twins, James and George, were only three, and Thomas, the baby, was only six months old.

Reuben came to the end of his row. It was a long way back along the next row of pollen-laden tassels of scraggly hill-country corn. And there were many more rows yet to be done. So he threw down his hoe, spoke no word to anyone, looked not back, but, in the expressive words of our chronicler for this period, "lit out" on foot for Knoxville.

M. Dumas, perhaps, would have liked to know how long this walk was, what adventures befell our hero on the way, and how he fared. A modern novelist would be curious to know more of the motives for this desertion of the family seat. Our chronicler throws no light on these problems. He merely states the fact. That Reuben was a person of impulse, of quick decision, and of action is apparent. Also, he had a rare independency of spirit— not so rare, perhaps in the Tennessee mountains—and was somewhat lacking in respect for constituted authority. We shall see that this action was characteristic.

Reuben's educational advantages had been slight. He was ill-fitted to make a living in the metropolis of eastern Tennessee—a very small town, we would judge it now, but appearing quite as large to him then as would Knoxville today to a youth from the hill country. We can well imagine him, tired and hungry, seeking out the one place in the city that had something of the atmosphere of the farm—the blacksmith shop. We can imagine Reuben sitting among the idlers that always congregated around blacksmith shops in the days when there were blacksmith shops, watching the smith hammering nails into shoes while he held between his legs and against his leathern apron a horse's hoof. But the capacity of the smith's mouth proves unequal to the task in hand.

"Shove me that box of nails, somebody. I need a couple more."

Quickly Reuben shoves the box to hand. The smith grunts approval.

"Wish I c'd ever of seen that boy Aleck move that fast. Long as that feller was here he never moved fast enough to pick up a hoss's hoof once he had him tech'd. Remember."

Apparently the crowd did, but Reuben walked over to a horse awaiting its turn to be shod, and, following the procedure he had observed the smith to use, picked up its hoof and lodged it between his knees in the prescribed manner.

"You seem to know horses, son."

"Well, no, suh, I don't. I never had a-hold of a horse before. But I know a little about mules."

"You wouldn't be in need of a job, would you?"

"I do need a job right smart. Have you got one?"

"Waal, mebbe. When could you start?"

"Right away. I'd sort of like something to eat first."

"When did you eat last?"

"It's been some spell. I don't just remember."

"Go on through and tell maw to fix you up. But don't loiter. You kin come right back and earn it."

In such manner Reuben Bernard began his apprenticeship at blacksmithing. Perhaps it seems a little informal for that remote period, but the blacksmith, whose name has been overlooked by the chronicler, and is not particularly important, evidently was among those not uncommon persons who desired to get much for little. In Reuben he had to admit he had found a bargain, for that youth's physique was fully up to the demands of blacksmithing,

1st Lieutenant Reuben F. Bernard, 1st Cavalry. Photograph taken at Washington, D. C., probably in 1864.

and he learned rapidly—perhaps too rapidly. It was not many months before Reuben had learned about all this tutor had to teach of the art that dates from Tubal Cain. There was some strange spark of ambition in this lad, not yet satisfied, nor likely to be by a career as blacksmith.

One day he chanced to see on the streets of Knoxville an imposing figure in blue wearing a cylindrical black and shining helmet surmounted by a waving plume, a long sabre hooked to his black belt. It is probable that Reuben had never seen a soldier before. Had he been better informed he might have known that the single row of nine gilt buttons equally spaced indicated a company officer and that the device of a six-pointed star and the orange facings of the uniform signified a member of one of the two dragoon regiments. You may be sure that Reuben stared at this impressive person, and you may be equally sure that it did not take much of a stare to attract the lieutenant's attention, for he was on recruiting service. In no short time Reuben was listening eagerly to the story of the glories of the mounted service, of the marches of the First Dragoons under its famous colonel, Stephen Watts Kearny, of the famous charge of Captain Charles May with the Second Dragoons at Resaca de la Palma in the last war, of the green colors of the Regiment of Mounted Riflemen, first at the gates of the City of Mexico, and the probability that Congress would shortly authorize new cavalry regiments, an assurance of rapid promotion and pay to all who would now unite their fortunes with those of the mounted branches of the United States Army.

"Do you mean that I might get to be an officer, like you?"

"Certainly. It is not uncommon for enlisted men to be commissioned from the ranks." He neglected to explain that fully qualified graduates of West Point were then accepting commissions as brevet second lieutenants because there were no vacancies. He would have been the more surprised of the two if it had been revealed to them that this raw back-country blacksmith would one day wear a brigadier general's star. You may be sure, however, that the lieutenant was more honest in promising a chance at fighting and adventure, although he felt that he was stretching a long bow when he promised Reuben a hundred battles. But this prediction also was to come true. Here was a recruiting officer who could not lie.

"But there is much more fighting since the last war," he explained. "And the mounted regiments are always in the Indian country—in Texas, New Mexico, Arizona, California, Oregon, Kansas, Nebraska, and Utah. There's always a chance of action in any of them. Of course, there is not much chance of a war, unless we fight Spain over Cuba"—a war Reuben was not to see until he was on the retired list. But these were the days of the "Ostend Manifesto." By this time you may be sure that Reuben was ready to sign his name on the dotted line.

"We're sending a small party of recruits to Jefferson Barracks tonight," the lieutenant explained. "We were about through here and most of the recruiting detail has gone on. But of course you will want a day or two."

"Not at all," Reuben replied. "I'm ready now."

And as a matter of fact he did not bother to quit his job at the blacksmith shop. He left Knoxville for Jefferson Barracks February 19, 1855, received recruit drill there until June, and then was assigned to the First Dragoons and left for New Mexico. Of course, there was no railroad. The detachment of one hundred and twenty-five recruits under command of a second lieutenant, M. T. Carr, went by steamer to Fort Leavenworth, Kansas, and marched on foot from there to Fort Riley in the same state. It is perhaps significant of the early recognition of Bernard's qualities of leadership that at this stage in the journey he was appointed lance sergeant and acting quartermaster sergeant of the detachment. At Fort Riley the recruits were mounted and the remainder of the journey to Fort Union, New Mexico, was made on horseback. There, at headquarters of the regiment, assignments to companies were made, and Bernard made a further march to Fort Craig, New Mexico. Lieutenant Carr was assigned to the same company, D of the First Dragoons. The entire trip had taken from June until October. On joining his company Bernard lost his temporary noncommissioned grade, but shortly after his arrival was appointed company blacksmith.

It was not until the following year that Bernard was able to chalk up Number One in his long list of fights, battles, skirmishes, and engagements, as they are variously listed in the official records. In March his company, under Lieutenant Carr, formed part of a considerable expedition under command of Captain D. T. Chandler of the Third Infantry against Navajo and Apache Indians, and his first fight was on the headwaters of the Gila River, March 28, 1856, followed shortly after by another on the Mimbres River, April 5th. In these years between the Mexican and Civil Wars there were many campaigns against the Navajoes, a tribe that never afterward caused any trouble. The Apaches, however, were perennial enemies, being almost the last of the Indian tribes to be subdued.

The army, when Bernard joined it, was entirely inadequate to its duties in protecting a recently extended Indian frontier. It consisted of something more than twelve thousand in the aggregate. There were ten regiments of infantry, two of which had been added in 1855. The four regiments of artillery each included two light or field batteries, the remaining ten companies serving in coast defense or in garrisoning posts, often acting as infantry. The year that Bernard enlisted, two regiments of "cavalry" were added to the army which previously had got along with two regiments of dragoons and one of mounted

Reuben Bernard saw an impressive figure in blue.

riflemen. Cavalry, dragoons and mounted riflemen were considered separate branches of service, but the distinction between them is not always clear—for example all were drilled by the same "Cavalry Tactics" of 1841. Dragoons were considered a sort of mounted infantry-of-the-line and were armed with musketoons, a short musket designed for volley firing, sabers and horse pistols. The mounted riflemen were rated as a mounted light infantry and omitted the sabers, but had percussion rifles and Colt's revolvers, both somewhat new to the army. Flintlocks had scarcely been discarded at the outbreak of the Civil War, and many of them were altered to take percussion caps and used in that conflict. The new cavalry regiments had rifle carbines, sabers and revolvers, and were supposed to do most of their fighting mounted. The tactics provided for drill with the lance, but none of our regiments seem ever to have been permanently equipped with that weapon.

While Bernard was still learning these things, his company was transferred from Fort Craig to Camp Moore, later named Fort Buchanan, in Arizona, forty-five miles southeast of Tucson, near the Mexican line. This area in 1856 was quite a bit wilder than the wild west we usually read about, and Bernard, shortly after his appointment as corporal in June, was given his first independent command, fifteen men, and sent in pursuit of a band of desperadoes who had murdered several Mexicans and stolen their pack trains. Bernard trailed the outlaws to Tubac, Arizona, surprised their camp, captured two of them, and recovered all of the stolen mules—no small success for a first venture. His reward was the command of a party of the same size in carrying the mail between Fort Buchanan and Fort Thorn, New Mexico, a distance of two hundred miles, inhabited only by hostile Indians. Eighteen times he made this ride without disaster, which would seem to be evidence that he had lost no time in learning the ways of the west. Early in 1858 he was taken sick and resigned as corporal, remaining in the post hospital for several months.

Meanwhile Company D was transferred to Fort Fillmore, New Mexico. About this time it came under the command of Second Lieutenant Richard S. C. Lord. Lord was graduated from West Point in 1852 and served for a short time in the Seventh Infantry and a considerable period in the Third Artillery before being transferred to the First Dragoons in 1857. One gathers from the record that Lieutenant Lord was not deficient in courage and that he probably was well versed in the art and science of war. But he seems to have been conspicuously lacking in that rare and indefinable necessity of the successful officer, leadership. And dragoons, from all accounts, were a pretty tough lot.

"What the devil can I do with this outfit?" he asked a brother officer on one occasion. "It's the most rag-tag and bob-tailed troop in the regiment."

"Well, if I were you I'd make that big blacksmith of yours first sergeant. He'll straighten things out."

"Bernard? Why, he's only a recruit in his first enlistment. They'll never stand for that."

"What's that got to do with it? You've got all the brains D troop needs. What you need is Bernard's fists. They're the biggest in the regiment."

Lord thought it over. He watched Bernard during an expedition in December, 1858, under command of Captain I. V. D. Reeve of the Eighth Infantry. There were actions in the Pinal Mountains on Christmas Day, on the San Carlos River two days later, and again in the Pinals, December 30th. The following March Bernard was again made corporal. In May he became sergeant. In June he was first sergeant.

There were a number of men in the company who did not like this arrangement. But not more than once did any one of them let his dissatisfaction be known. At the first quibble about an order from the first sergeant, the offender found himself on the ground. Bernard was quick in action and his fists landed like pile drivers. Perhaps this manner of enforcing discipline was not strictly according to regulations, but officers could be conveniently blind at times.

During 1859 the company was returned to Fort Buchanan and from there moved to Fort Breckinridge, Arizona, where it remained until the outbreak of the Civil

War. In the fall Lieutenant Lord led the company on a ten-day scout, during which there was a fight with Apaches on the San Pedro River, November 9th. While in camp forty miles north of Tucson, Bernard reënlisted and was reappointed first sergeant. Several times he was on detached service in command of a separate detachment. In January, 1860, with fifteen men he pursued a party of Indians who had stolen stock from ranchers, recovered the stock, and was complimented in post orders for the exploit.

During 1860 he was granted a furlough. One can imagine that he strutted when he arrived home, a returning prodigal, wearing the orange-striped uniform of a first sergeant of dragoons. Younger brothers and sisters begged for Indian stories and learned something of army life on the frontier. At least three of the boys went into military service in the war that was soon to come.

In 1860 a uniform was not as common as it soon became, and Bernard found himself more conspicuous than he desired to be. So at times he wore civilian attire, and was so dressed on a certain visit to old friends in Knoxville. That was the summer of the four-cornered political campaign in which the new Republican party, with Abraham Lincoln as its candidate, was victorious over the divided democracy represented by Douglas, Breckinridge, and Bell. The Lincoln campaign was not carried on in the South excepting in the border sections, but there was some Republican following in eastern Tennessee. The tall stove-pipe hat favored by Mr. Lincoln became in a sense the mark of his adherents, just as the brown derby represented Alfred E. Smith in the 1928 campaign. In some manner Bernard acquired one of these stove-pipe hats and his Knoxville friends dared him to wear it to a Democratic meeting to be held in the open. Bernard had no large interest in politics, but slavery was not an institution that had ever done him any good, and he did not desire to see it extended to New Mexico and the other territories with which he was familiar. He was, if anything, a Republican, and that the new party was not over popular in his home bailiwick probably made him more partisan than he otherwise would have been. He would always take a dare, so he wore the hat.

Before the public speaking began a big fellow possessed of considerable alcoholic courage was marching up and down parading his politics and challenging anyone who did not like his appearance or his opinions to fight it out. He spied Bernard's tall hat and made for the soldier. Bernard refused to give ground.

"I suppose you with your stove-pipe hat would like to settle matters with me—" he shouted, and without another word smashed the hat down over Bernard's eyes and ears. The crowd roared with laughter, and it took Bernard some minutes to get out of the hat. Madly he clawed at it and at last tore it off in pieces, and came out with his arms swinging. The other man was big, but Bernard was stronger—and tougher. The drunk kept his feet long enough to receive blow after blow, and to return some of them with interest, but at last he went down for a clean knockout. It was the only Republican victory in Tennessee in 1860.

II

AT APACHE PASS*

SERGEANT BERNARD returned from his furlough a marked figure in his regiment. He had been generally successful in several independent forays and he was a bit cocky over them. His spirit of independence was no whit lessened by the fact that he was almost immediately sent to Fort Buchanan in charge of a cavalry detachment of a dozen men. Fort Buchanan had been slated to become a six company post and already was commanded by a lieutenant colonel, Pitcairn Morrison of the Seventh Infantry, but at this time only two companies, C and E, of that regiment were in garrison there. It was customary to have some cavalry at every post, when practicable, because a mounted detachment could have some chance of running down raiding parties of Indians, and was extremely valuable in the scouting, patrolling and escort duty that fell to the lot of a frontier garrison in those days.

In fact, no sooner did Bernard's detachment arrive than it was sent out on one of these investigative "pursue and

---

*This is frankly a reconstruction of a controversial episode. However no statement is made that is not based upon evidence. The primary sources are "The Apache Pass Fight," by Brigadier General B. J. D. Irwin, in the *Infantry Journal*, April, 1928; "A True History of the Outbreak of the Noted Apache Chieftain Cochise in the Year 1861," by W. S. Oury in the *Arizona Star*, June 28, 1877; an interview with "Policeman Oberly, of Brooklyn," in an unidentified New York newspaper of 1887; and Bernard's report at Camp Bowie March 23, 1869 (quoted in Chapter V. *infra*). Secondary accounts that mention Bernard's part in the affair are "Apache, Past and Present," by C. T. Connell in *Tucson Citizen*, beginning March 27, 1921; *History of Arizona*, by T. E. Farish, Vol. II, Chapter II (Phoenix, 1915-18); *Pioneer Days in Arizona*, by Frank C. Lockwood (New York, 1932); *Arizona*, by James H. McClintock, Vol. I, pp. 179-182 (Chicago, 1919); and *The Story of Arizona*, by Will H. Robinson (Phoenix, 1919).

punish" affairs. Colonel Morrison had been waiting since October for a force available to send out, and it was now February. Of course the occasion was not very important, or he would not have waited so long, but he had been much pestered by the victim of an Apache foray and he welcomed the opportunity to make some show of action. This unimportant raid brings together two highly dramatic and debatable episodes in Arizona history.

The first had its beginning in Mexico some twelve years before. On September 30, 1849, a party of Mexicans left Santa Cruz, Sonora, for Magdalena to attend there the fiesta of San Francisco. In this party were Inez Gonzales, a young and beautiful Mexican girl, and her fiance, Lieutenant Limon. They were accompanied by her uncle, her aunt, Mercedes Pacheco, a female servant, Jesus Salvador, and eight soldiers. In the Cocospera Canyon the party was ambushed by a band of Pinal Apaches, said to have been led by Es-kim-in-zin, a chief who caused much trouble for Major General George Crook during his command in Arizona in the middle seventies.

It was a bloody fight. Lieutenant Limon and his eight men were killed, as was the uncle. The three women were captured. Mercedes Pacheco was sold by the Apaches to a band of Navajoes and was never again heard of. Inez Gonzales was sold to two Santa Fe traders, Peter Blacklaws and Pedro Acheveque, from whom she was rescued by John R. Bartlett, United States boundary commissioner.

Jesus Salvador, the servant, delayed her escape too long. To her and one of her captors was born a son who later became known widely, but not well, as Mickey Free, sometimes scout and guide, and described in his declining years as a "wandering, aged, unkempt dependent of the government, an Apache in nature, in cunning, in mind,

[15]

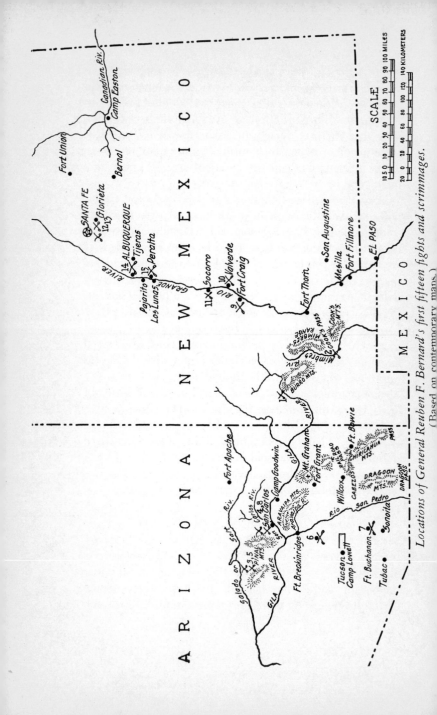

Locations of General Reuben F. Bernard's first fifteen fights and scrimmages.
(Based on contemporary maps.)

and in action." She escaped in 1855 and in 1860 with her
boy, then six years of age, was living at the ranch of John
Ward in the Sonoita Valley about twelve miles from Fort
Buchanan. The histories of Arizona euphemistically
state that she was Ward's housekeeper. Ward also has
some note in Arizona annals as scout and guide, but most
of the references to him are similarly lacking in compliment. He seems to have been genuinely fond of the boy.

In October, 1860, a band of Apaches—whether Coyo-
teros, Pinals or Chiricahuas is not clear from the evidence
—descended on Ward's ranch in his absence and carried
off some work oxen, horses, a burro and the boy Mickey
who was guarding them. When Ward returned he followed
the trail to the San Pedro River. Here he became convinced
that the marauders were Chiricahuas headed by Cochise.
Cochise, whose name also appears as Cachise, Cocheis,
Coches, Kuchies, Ka Kreese, and several other variants,
of which the first has gained currency as the name of a
large Arizona county, was hereditary chief of the Chiricahuas, and in later times became a very famous Indian.
He is described by Brigadier General B. J. D. Irwin as
"then in the prime of life; tall and well favored in face
and figure; about thirty years old and at least six feet
in height. His presence was bold and warlike; presenting
the attributes of a superb specimen of robust, physical
manhood." He "had always been at peace with the
whites," according to Bernard, although other accounts say
he took part in the earlier warfare of Mangas Coloradas
but made peace in 1856 and had not been on the war-
path since. General Irwin, who characterizes Apache
Indians at large as "one and all . . . alike; treacherous,
bloodthirsty, and cowardly, and ever on the alert to ambush small parties of incautious travelers," declares that
the highway leading to and from Apache Pass, Cochise's

stronghold, was "dotted with the graves or stone tumuli that covered the remains of the victims of his treachery."

We can be sure this was Ward's opinion as he haunted the post during the winter clamoring for the recovery of the boy and vengeance against Cochise. Early in February, 1861, Bernard's dragoons were turned out on this errand. Colonel Morrison assigned the command to one of his officers, Second Lieutenant George Nicholas Bascom, a native of Kentucky and West Point graduate of the class of 1858. Bascom had not distinguished himself at the Military Academy nor in his three years in the army; he had had very little Indian experience, but he seems to have been generally well-liked by his associates, and, after his death at the battle of Valverde a year later, a fort was named in his honor in New Mexico. He has gone down in most Arizona histories as the villain in the piece that follows, not altogether fairly, and he has his warm defenders to this day.

The expedition arrived at the stage station of the Great Overland Mail line of Butterfield & Company in Apache Pass on February 5th. Telling the station keeper, Culver, that they were marching for the Rio Grande, Bascom moved down the canyon about three-quarters of a mile and went into camp.

Apache Pass is in a gloomy region, much cut up with many small ravines, and traversed, at this period, by a steep and rugged semblance of a road. There are some clear mountain springs near by, which made the place almost an oasis in this section of Arizona despite its otherwise unprepossessing appearance. The pass itself is so steep that one traveler thought it more nearly resembled a peak. The events now about to occur have given it a reputation in keeping with its nature.

Cochise had seen the troops go by, and he now approached the stage station to ask his friends there what the armed party was after. Culver told the chief what the officer had said, so the Indian went on to the camp to pay the usual ceremonial visit, no doubt expecting the usual reward, something to eat and perhaps some tobacco or other small present. With him were three warriors, a woman and a boy.

In the officer's tent were Lieutenant Bascom, Ward, and an interpreter, Antonio.

"There comes Cochise," whispered Ward.

"All right. Go tell Sergeant Robinson there to get some of the men and surround the tent. We may have trouble." Ward went out on this errand, and Cochise and his party stalked into the tent. They were given something to eat, and some desultory conversation was carried on through the interpreter. At last, when the lieutenant saw that several soldiers were at hand he began to talk seriously.

"Cochise, we want the boy that was taken from Mr. Ward's ranch."

"He say, 'What boy look like?' " said Antonio, interpreting. Bascom described the boy.

"He say he know nothing about such a boy. He say he send out, ask if any of his warriors see boy like that. He say he can find boy anywhere he bring him in."

"Tell him that won't do. Tell him we know he has the boy, and that we will keep him and all these people here until that boy is produced."

But as Antonio translated these words, Cochise sprang from his place, drew a long knife, and slashed open the side of the tent; his head followed immediately the stroke of the knife and with almost a single motion he leaped outside amid the astonished soldiers and dashed past them before a weapon could be raised against him.

Cochise sprang from his place, drew a long knife.

Cochise's brother and two nephews attempted to follow, but the soldiers had collected their wits by this time and one Indian was knocked down with the butt of a carbine while another was transfixed by a bayonet — a wound which curiously did not prove serious. Cochise was safely away.

Bernard, at the other end of camp caring for his horse, came dashing back at the sound of the commotion and the scattering shots fired vainly after the fugitive.

"Turn out the detachment, Sergeant," the lieutenant shouted. "Cochise has got away. We must go after him."

Bernard, of course, got his men into action as quickly as possible. Inwardly he was fuming. From what he heard of the matter, the attempt to seize Cochise appeared to be a violation of hospitality. Moreover, it had failed, and that was unforgivable. But he said nothing, except to offer a suggestion.

"Perhaps, sir, we could go by the stage station to warn the people there of what has happened."

"A very good idea, sergeant. Lead on."

Bernard led the detachment at a fast pace. But even so he was too late.

Cochise, a few minutes before had appeared before the stage station with several of his warriors. He had beckoned to the men there to come out to a parley with him. Culver, the station agent, Wallace, a driver, and Walsh, a hostler, had known the chief a long while and had no suspicion that anything was wrong. They walked out, in their shirt sleeves, to where he was, and began talking. Several of the warriors sidled behind the men, and at a signal from Cochise, made a rush at them and seized the three. Walsh and Culver, big athletic men, struggled and thrashed about, knocking over several of their assailants, and broke away. The Indians opened fire. A bullet struck Culver just as he reached the station and he fell through the door. At this moment the troopers arrived. Bascom and two or three soldiers rushed to the aid of Culver and dragged him through the door, while the rest of the detachment scattered through the corral. At this moment Walsh reached the stone wall in rear of the house, but as his head appeared over its top, a trooper fired, mistaking him for an Indian, and the hostler was killed. As soon as the Apaches saw the troops they fled, taking Wallace with them, a prisoner.

Cochise was on the war-path. More and more of his followers joined him. A short distance away they saw the campfires of a train of nine wagons that had halted for the night on an eastward journey through the pass. In a silent, stealthy ambush the Chiricahuas captured the entire party. Eight New Mexicans of Spanish descent were tied to their own wagon wheels and burned to death in the destruction of their train. Two Americans named Jordan and Lyons were held as prisoners for more refined tortures.

But there is more blood to shed. The stage-coach from Tuscon is approaching the pass. The ambushed Indians fire a volley, breaking the leg of the driver, King Lyons, and killing one of the lead mules. Passengers leap from the coach and cut away the harness of the dead animal. William Buckley, superintendent of the line, seizes the reins, and the coach speeds on. Just ahead is a steep pitch of the road into a rocky ravine crossed by a narrow bridge. Cochise has had time to throw down both sides of the stone bridge, but, fortunately for the coach passengers the middle has not been destroyed. The flying mules, dashing down the steep descent, huddle a second and leap the narrow gulch; their velocity slides the axles across the bridge while the wheels hang free on both sides. By some lucky chance the wheels take hold again without an upset, and the stage coach flies on to the station, in front of which a mule falls dead, an accident that would have meant the death of nine persons had it occurred at any earlier stage of the dash through the ambush.

That night Superintendent Buckley sent a courier back to Tucson, asking William S. Oury, agent of the line there, to call on Fort Breckinridge for aid. This resulted in the ordering out of Company D, under Lieutenant Lord, and Company G, under First Lieutenant Isaiah N. Moore, of the First Dragoons. Meanwhile Lieutenant Bascom also had sent a courier, to Fort Buchanan, particularly for medical aid. This soldier led a mule up the mountainside, traveled all night to the mail station at

Dragoon Spring, got a remount there, and arrived at the fort the second night of his journey.

Bernard John Dowling Irwin, then assistant surgeon at Fort Buchanan, later brigadier general, volunteered to go to Apache Pass direct, instead of attempting to join the dragoons coming from Fort Breckinridge. Fourteen infantrymen were assigned to accompany him, and James Graydon, a discharged soldier, volunteered to go along. The trip took two days, and on the second day, while crossing the broad plain west of the Chiricahua mountain range, a party of Indians, evidently returning from a raid, was discovered driving a herd of cattle and horses. The surgeon immediately led his escort on an attack on this party, and, during a running fight of several miles, the stock was recovered and three Indians were captured. A medal of honor was awarded to Irwin for this exploit. Unknown to him at that time, however, he was aided by the presence of Company B of the Eighth Infantry that happened to be marching by within sight of the Indians. The infantrymen, on their way from Fort Breckinridge to Fort Bliss, had no part in the further events at the Pass, and, in fact, did not know that their march had helped Irwin.

But no chance help came to the small party now besieged at the stage station. On the night of his capture Wallace was brought under guard to within sight of the troops. A stick was set up and a paper placed in its split end. A daring trooper crawled out after the Indians had left and brought in the message. Wallace had written in charcoal at Cochise's dictation, "Treat my people well and I will do the same by yours, of whom I have three." This was the first intimation to the troops of the capture of the two men at the wagon train.

The next morning the troopers and the stage employes

drove their stock to a spring about six hundred yards west of the station for watering. As they were returning, a burst of shots warned them that they were ambushed. Moses Lyons, a stage employe, was killed at the first fire, and another employe and a soldier were wounded. In the confusion the stock stampeded and got away.

The following afternoon, Wallace again was seen approaching under Indian guard. His hands were tied behind him, and, still in his shirt sleeves, he was shivering with cold. His escort slipped into a ravine leading toward the station, and allowed the prisoner to advance the length of a long rope that they had tied to the bonds which held his hands. Wallace called for the lieutenant. Bascom and Bernard approached.

"Cochise says that if you will free the Indians you have taken, he will let me go," Wallace said.

"Does he still have the other two white men mentioned in the note?"

"Yes, but I have not seen much of them. I have been tied up like this for two days; I am starved and freezing. I do not know if they have been tortured."

"Tell Cochise that I will free all the Indians if he will release you and the two other men."

Wallace turned to confer with his hidden captors. Bernard broke in.

"Lieutenant, for God's sake, if he won't free all of them, take him up on Wallace. One white man's worth a dozen lousy Indians, and we can always kill a few more."

"That would hardly be fair, Sergeant. As it is, it's three warriors, with a woman and boy thrown in, for three white men, and they non-combatants."

By this time Wallace had his answer.

Bernard led the detachment at a fast pace.

"I'm sorry, Lieutenant, but Cochise sticks to his original offer. He says he can't include the other two."

"Accept, Lieutenant. Save this poor devil," Bernard insisted. "It's the only way you can do anything for those other fellows anyhow. And I tell you, sir, it is unusual for an Indian to offer this much. An Apache chief has not such power as you think. If these men were captured by other warriors, he cannot compel them to give up their prisoners. No doubt he has tried. But he knows and likes Wallace and is trying to save him."

"No, Sergeant, I cannot do it. I can't be unfair to those two men. They are all in the same boat and must all take their chances together."

"Damn it, Lieutenant, here's a man whose life is at stake."

"You forget yourself, Sergeant. I tell you it can't be done that way."

"To hell with regulations, sir, do you know what those fiends will do to this poor fellow? Have you ever seen what's left when they get through with their torturing? Damn it, I say accept."

[25]

"Sergeant, you are insubordinate. Consider yourself under arrest. Please to remember that I command here. Wallace, I'm sorry, but my offer also stands. Tell Cochise if he will bring his three prisoners to me, I will release those I hold. That's all I can say."

"Please, sir,—"

"I'm sorry, Wallace, but that is final."

As the parley ended, a jerk of the rope brought Wallace to the ground, and he was dragged back over the sharp stones to the ravine. He was never seen alive again. He was immediately dragged to death behind the horse of Cochise.

The first relief party to arrive was Irwin's detachment, followed within a few hours by the two troops of the First Dragoons. The next morning a scout was undertaken, but nothing could be seen of the Apaches. The wreck of the wagon train was found, and the grisly remains of its people. The troopers spurred on in search of Cochise's village. A flock of buzzards was disturbed, and soldiers rode to investigate. They found three bodies, littered with lance holes. One of these was identified by Oury of the stage line as Wallace, although he could only be certain by the gold filling of the teeth. The others presumably were Jordan and Lyons. Burning to avenge their deaths, the scouting party rode on and found Cochise's camp, but the Apaches were gone. The abandoned camp was burned.

There was nothing more to do. Thwarted and angry the men turned back to the station. Among the soldiers arose some discussion as to the prisoners. "Hang them. Burn them," was the bitter demand. "Well, why not," said the officers.

"I captured three, and I propose to hang them as an object lesson for these devils," the doughty surgeon insisted. Lieutenant Moore, the senior officer, agreed.

When the party returned to camp, Lieutenant Moore told Bascom what had been decided. He demurred. The Indians were prisoners of war. Irwin insisted on his right to dispose of those he had taken. Moore said that he would assume full responsibility.

The next morning the troops prepared to leave the bloody scene. They marched forth, with their six Indian prisoners, including the one who had been bayonetted in the first attempt to escape. He had now nearly recovered. A tree shaded the new-made grave where Wallace and his companions had been buried, and to this tree were hanged the six captives. For many months their bodies swung there, an unheeded warning.

The troops separated and returned to their stations. The Indian woman and boy were taken to Fort Buchanan and there released. Irwin and Bascom were commended in orders, and specifically the hanging of the Indians was approved.

There remained the trial of First Sergeant Bernard. The charges were not pushed vigorously. It was the spring of 1861, and there were more important events than the court-martial of a non-commissioned officer to worry about. Bernard was acquitted.

III

THE CIVIL WAR IN NEW MEXICO*

THE regular army in the spring of 1861 was not well placed for the suppression of rebellion and insurrection. No one of its nineteen regiments was assembled. Its two hundred companies were scattered in some eighty-eight posts in twenty states. In February Brigadier General David E. Twiggs surrendered the Department of Texas—nineteen posts—to the secession element in that state. Some of the organizations refused to recognize the surrender and a number of them escaped north before the firing on Fort Sumter. The garrisons of the Territory of New Mexico, then including Arizona, were left isolated.

As soon as it became evident that there was to be war, a force of Texas troops under Lieutenant Colonel John R. Baylor moved into the valley of the Rio Grande in New Mexico to take possession of what the Confederacy had proclaimed as the Territory of Arizona. Bernard's troop, D, with its squadron-companion, G, both under the command of Captain I. N. Moore of the First Dragoons, destroyed and abandoned Fort Breckinridge, marched to Fort Buchanan and destroyed it, and were on their way to oppose the invasion when they learned that Baylor had defeated companies of the Mounted Riflemen and Seventh Infantry at Mesilla and that the Union force had surrendered at San Augustine Springs.

These repeated surrenders of regular forces had caused

---

*The finding of the court of inquiry called at the request of Captain Lord will be found in *War of the Rebellion Records,* Series I, Volume 9, which volume contains other records of the New Mexico campaign. See also *Colorado Volunteers in the Civil War,* by W. C. Whitford (Denver, 1906).

enlisted men of the regular army, who were almost solidly loyal to the Union, to distrust their officers. Captain Moore, however, gave no occasion for suspicion. Immediately he destroyed his baggage train and led his two troops into the mountains, taking a roundabout course from Cook's Pass to Fort Craig on the Rio Grande where Colonel B. S. Roberts of the Mounted Riflemen was attempting to conserve the relics of the regular army in the southwest, which totaled eleven companies of infantry of the Fifth, Seventh and Tenth Regiments, and four mounted companies of the Second Dragoons and Mounted Riflemen, when Moore's dragoons arrived. Five regiments of New Mexico Volunteers were being organized, one of them commanded by the famous scout Kit Carson. Colorado Volunteers were on the way. Edward R. S. Canby, recently appointed colonel of the newly authorized Nineteenth Infantry, was sent to command the department.

Meanwhile the rest of the First Dragoons was assembled at Washington and assigned to the Army of the Potomac. It was newly designated the First Cavalry, the number it holds today as the first cavalry regiment in the United States Army to be mechanized. Its New Mexico troops, D and G, were assigned as bodyguard to Colonel Canby. This was Bernard's first contact with Canby, under whom he was to serve in more than one campaign. Canby evidently was favorably impressed by the former blacksmith, for Bernard was among non-commissioned officers recommended for commissions and immediately appointed acting second lieutenants. But it so happened that Acting Lieutenant Bernard was ordered to report to recently promoted Captain R. S. C. Lord, officially commanding the old company, D, now of the First Cavalry.

The Confederacy also was organizing and in February, 1862, Brigadier General Henry H. Sibley, once briefly a major of the First Dragoons, led a considerable force of Texas troops against Fort Craig. A demonstration from the opposite bank of the Rio Grande did little damage except to disorganize one of the newly formed regiments of New Mexico Volunteers and confirm Canby in an impression that his reinforcement was none too reliable. Sibley moved up the river and attempted a crossing at Valverde February 21st. An improvised battery manned by Companies G of the Second Cavalry and I of the Third Cavalry under Captain Alexander McRae, a North Carolinian, disputed the crossing. A Texas charge drove back McRae's battery a short distance, but a countercharge was made by the regular infantry and cavalry which cleared the crossing and drove the Confederates back to a dry bed of the Rio Grande in rear. There was now some see-sawing which had the effect of bringing on a general engagement, about the last thing Colonel Canby wanted. When he arrived on the field McRae's battery was holding the right, a battery of two 24-pound howitzers held the left, while the center drooped back disconsolately in the direction of the supine Second New Mexico. Kit Carson's First New Mexico was valiantly in the fight, as was a single company present of Colorado Volunteers and Graydon's very "Independent Spy Company." The regular infantry and cavalry were backing the howitzers but McRae's support had thinned out so that a detachment of Texas Rangers was able to charge over his battery and the loyal North Carolinian was killed across one of his guns. The right of the Union line was then in the air, and Canby made a hurried withdrawal to Fort Craig. Sibley summoned the fort to surrender, but Canby refused to adopt the surrendering habit. The Confederates had had quite enough of fighting and withdrew toward Albuquerque and Santa Fe.

That afternoon Colonel Canby sent for certain officers. It is even possible to give their names—Captain George W. Howland, and Acting Lieutenants Richard Wall and John Falvey, all of the Third Cavalry, Captain Lord and Acting Lieutenant Bernard of the First Cavalry, and Ira W. Claflin, recently promoted first lieutenant in the newly organized Sixth Cavalry. To them the commanding officer explained that the Confederate force was retreating toward Albuquerque and Santa Fe because of lack of supplies, and that they probably would attempt the capture of Fort Union to the northeast, where enough supplies were stored to outfit several armies the size of any that so far had operated in New Mexico.

"Gentlemen, we must hold Fort Union. If we can do that our setback at the Valverde crossing is of no importance. I have received word that a regiment of Colorado Volunteers is on the way, but it may arrive too late. I want you, Captain Howland, and you, Captain Lord, to move your squadrons, by separate routes, around these rebels and beat them to Fort Union. If one of you gets through I believe the fort will be safe. If both of you get through, I know it will. Captain Howland, how many of your men are fit for an arduous march?"

"Since the fighting, sir, I have twenty-eight men of C, ten of K, six of D, and six of G, a total of fifty for duty."

"And you, Captain Lord, have about the same number in your squadron, I believe."

"Exactly, sir. Fifty men present for duty in Companies D and G."

"Captain Howland has two lieutenants. You, Captain Lord, have only Acting Lieutenant Bernard, so I am attaching Mr. Claflin, who has volunteered for this duty as it probably will be easier for him to join his regiment in the East from Fort Union than from here."

Colonel Canby then prescribed the routes to be taken by the two parties, assigned guides, and gave other necessary instruction. Early that evening Howland's squadron slipped away form Fort Craig and soon was lost in the dusk. Lord's squadron left a short time later. All night D and G rode in the broken country west of the Rio Grande. All the next day and the next night they pushed on with only brief halts. In the mountains near Socorro they met and scattered a band of Indians in a brief skirmish. But now came the more perilous part of their mission. It was necessary to turn to the east and cross the upper waters of the Rio Grande ahead of Sibley's army if the objective was to be reached in time. As they approached the river at Pardes (probably Pajarito) they met an unexpected obstacle. A February thaw had filled the river with ice, and it was running high, seemingly impassible. Scouting parties were sent north and south along the valley trail. To the south the Confederates had reached Los Lunas, twelve miles away. To the north twelve miles Albuquerque was occupied in force.

Here was a problem not contained in the books of tactics studied by Captain Lord at West Point. As he saw it, he was trapped between an overwhelmingly superior force of the enemy and an impassible river. Even if he could cross, it would be only to fall into the hands of many more Confederates than he could successfully fight. If he stayed where he was, surrender was only a matter of hours. In fact, surrender seemed the end in either alternative. As to his own force, he had fifty unfed men, fifty broken-down horses, and a lightly loaded pack train of very tired mules. In addition to all that, he had just discovered that his guides had disappeared. He mentioned these circumstances to his lieutenants. But Bernard, now being one of them, could speak up.

"There has been enough surrendering in this campaign. I'll never allow an enlisted man to be surrendered without his consent, while I am an officer."

"But Lieutenant Claflin will agree that to make a dangerous crossing in the face of the enemy violates a cardinal principle of —" And the argument went on, neither Lord nor Claflin noticing that Bernard was no longer there to hear it. They were startled within a few minutes to hear the sharp-barked command,

"Prepare to mount. Mount."

"What is Bernard up to?" The captain's tone showed annoyance.

"Probably getting the troop ready for whatever we may decide."

But Bernard was saying this:

"Men, we were ordered by Colonel Canby to go to Fort Union. Fort Union is over that way. There are a lot of rebels across the river. I don't know how many, and I don't care. I'm going across that river and I am going to keep on until I am stopped. If any of you want to come along, come ahead. Those who stay here with Captain Lord will probably be surrendered to the rebels we fought the other day."

Not a command was given. But as Bernard turned and dashed into the river, the well-trained squadron broke by twos as prescribed in tactics for passing an obstacle and followed. Not a man fell out.

"Stop that blasted fool," Captain Lord shouted to Claflin. But the lieutenant restrained him.

"It's too late now sir, they are in the water. You might as well let them try it."

Soon the tired horses were fighting for their lives, swimming in the swirling water, buffeted by crumbling ice cakes, many of them cut by the sharp edges of the

"Let them go," Bernard shouted to the men. "Save yourselves."

floes leaving quickly-washed-away traces of blood in the water, plunging, but with heads kept up by expert riders who swam beside them. Bernard reached the other shore and turned to help those who were in trouble. Only cavalry horses, trained to follow in line, could have made it, as was soon demonstrated: for the pack train, guided by courageous enlisted men who did not propose to be left behind, followed on the heels of the mounted men. In a few minutes the mules stampeded. Struck by ice cakes, the tormented and unmanageable animals turned tail and were swept downstream.

"Let them go," Bernard shouted to the men. "Save yourselves."

Not a man was lost. Not a mule was saved.

Lord was not lacking in courage, as he was to prove again and again before the war was over. Once shown the way, he was able to follow. Perhaps anger over Bernard's summary action spurred him on. In a few moments the captain and Claflin were with the squadron.

"Lieutenant Bernard, I will hold you responsible for the loss of those mules and every article they carried."

"Then we will find out if it is more important to lose something in trying to save everything, or to lose everything by lying down like a whipped cur. Try to surrender this outfit now and I'll prefer charges of treason against you."

"Lieutenant Bernard, you are insubordinate. Consider yourself under —"

"Wait a moment, Captain, please," Lieutenant Claflin broke in. "This can all be settled later. Now that we are across the river, it seems to me the important thing is to go on to Fort Union, as we were ordered."

"But how. We have no guides."

"We will find the way. If you will order an advance on

Fort Union I will accept your orders," Bernard conceded. Both officers had cooled down somewhat, and both were sensible enough to realize that the situation was too serious to admit of personal wrangling. Lord realized that Bernard's audacity and leadership had accomplished a crossing. Bernard did not really believe that Lord had contemplated treason, but had little faith in the captain's ability in time of stress. Personal hostilities were suspended and those with the enemy resumed. Bernard had not awaited the captain's arrival to send out scouts, who now reported, and the acting lieutenant, in a manner preserving all the niceties of military etiquette that would be expected of a first sergeant, suggested a course of action that Captain Lord thought it well to order. The result was the surprise of a Confederate outpost at Tejaras Pass and the capture of a lieutenant and fourteen men. The squadron then moved rapidly toward Fort Union, reaching that post without further adventure. Within a few hours Howland's command arrived: it also had had its troubles, including a skirmish at Comanche Canyon.

A few days later, on March 10th, Colonel John P. Slough arrived at Fort Union with his First Colorado Regiment of Volunteer Infantry, and assumed command. For unknown reasons probably connected with local politics, Colonel Slough apparently was never hailed as a Colorado war hero, yet his actions in this campaign seem generally to have been commendable. He could well have awaited attack at the fort, but he took the aggressive immediately in an offensive against Santa Fe and Albuquerque. Only eleven days after his arrival he marched out with his regiment, an additional independent company of Colorado Volunteers, the Fourth Regiment of New Mexico Volunteers, the two cavalry squadrons from Fort Craig and an additional company, E, of the Third Cavalry, Companies A and G of the Fifth Infantry, and two light batteries of four guns each, his force totaling one thousand, three hundred and forty-two.

Three days later he detached as an advance guard or maneuvering force about one-third of his column—four companies of Colorado Volunteers, the squadrons of Captains Lord and Howland, and E of the Third Cavalry, a total of four hundred and eighteen men—under Major John M. Chivington. This Major Chivington is one whose name persists in the annals of the West, for he has the dubious fame of being in command at the Indian battle that has become known as the Sand Creek Massacre. There are those who deny that whole kindergartens of Indian babies were killed on Sand Creek and there are others who say there was no such slaughter of the innocents since the time of King Herod. The truth of that much debated affair does not concern us here. It is sufficient to note that this was, in truth, the Chivington of Sand Creek.

Chivington's force left Bernal Springs at three o'clock the afternoon of March 25th; by midnight he had marched thirty-five miles—a considerable hike for recently enlisted volunteers—and encamped on the farm of one Alexander Valle, the farm being known as Pigeon's Ranch, it is said because of the dexterity of its owner in "cutting a pigeon's wing" in the barn dances or whatever it was they were having in New Mexico at that time. Near the ranch was La Glorietta Pass opening into the Apache Canyon. After a two-hour rest, a scouting party was sent out into Glorietta and at ten o'clock the next morning pickets of the enemy were surprised in Apache Canyon. This proved to be the advance guard of General Sibley's Confederates marching to the attack on Fort Union and the encounter was unexpected on both sides.

Chivington immediately ordered forward his entire command and the Confederates opened up with two howitzers. Chivington realized that howitzers could not climb mountains conveniently, so he deployed two companies of his Colorado infantry to the left and a single company to the right, holding his cavalry ready for a charge. To avoid being flanked, the Confederates fell back a mile and a half. Chivington followed and called the same play, but this time dismounting the regular cavalry, much to the disgust of its officers.

The relations of Captain Lord and his lieutenant had been coldly distant. Needless to say, they had not aired their differences before any of the officers of volunteers who were their technical superiors.

But the sound of rifle fire made Bernard fidget.

"When are we going to get into it?" he inquired, not particularly of Captain Lord.

"It looks like a volunteer benefit," Lord answered. "Look, he's sending in his Colorado cavalry now. I suppose he has read the tactics and thinks that dragoons are not supposed to fight mounted."

"But I think we were expected to follow along, Captain," Howland remarked.

"The devil with what he expects. I want orders before I move any of my men into such an affair as this."

"But this is a battle," Bernard remarked, dryly.

"Lieutenant Bernard is itching to get into it I see," Howland observed. "And I'm inclined to agree with him, even if it is a Colorado show. If you have no particular use for Lieutenant Bernard for a few minutes, would you loan him to me, Captain Lord? Maybe we can stir up a little fun, and show these greenhorns how to fight."

"None of my men will move without orders," replied

Lord, coldly. "But orders do not seem to worry Lieutenant Bernard much, so he can do as he pleases."

"That will do you for permission, Bernard. Take C troop and see what you can do with it. I'll follow along."

The Colorado cavalry had charged when the double flanking move appeared to be near success, and had run over and trampled the enemy under the horses' hoofs. Now Captain Downing's Colorado company and Lieutenant Bernard with C of the Third Cavalry, poured in so sharp a fire from the right that the Confederates were driven up a canyon on the left side of the main canyon, where a large number of prisoners were taken by the flanking infantry companies. The Confederate line was now in confusion and decided generally that its presence was no longer required. Chivington fell back on Pigeon's Ranch.

After the Apache Canyon skirmish, both sides brought forward their main forces. Colonel Slough, arriving at Pigeon's Ranch, sent Chivington's force on an end run to the left, to do some more mountain climbing. But Sibley now took the offensive and brought the fighting forward to the vicinity of Glorietta Pass and Pigeon's Ranch. 'At first the two federal batteries were driven back. Artillery duelling followed. Then the Texans charged again and again, but the batteries commanded by Captain John F. Ritter of the Fifth Infantry, and Lieutenant Claflin continued to discourage them with grape, cannister and shell, even after Colonel Slough, for some unexplained reason, ordered a retreat. Ritter fired a few final volleys, coolly limbered up his guns, and followed the rest of the Union army.

But meanwhile Chivington's force, from a height of a thousand feet, had charged down the mountainside, arriving in the rear of the Confederate position after seizing one six-pounder gun, which was spiked, in the midst of eighty-five wagons, which were burned, and five or six hundred horses, which were killed. Chivington then went back the way he had come, rejoined Colonel Slough, and the entire outfit moved back in the direction of Fort Union as far as Tejaras Pass. Bernard, being of little value to Captain Lord, but of immense value to anyone else, was given charge of the prisoners, some eighty-eight, took them to Fort Union, and returned to Tejaras Pass with his escort.

One wonders if it were luck or sense that had caused Colonel Slough to lose a battle, but win a campaign. The destruction of the supply train and animals was decisive in the war in New Mexico. General Sibley retreated rapidly, not even stopping at Santa Fe. Colonel Canby fell upon the Confederate army at Albuquerque and bombarded it for two days. But not being strong enough to make an assault, Canby moved north, made a junction at Tejaras Pass with the, perhaps accidental, victors of the Battle of Glorietta or Pigeon's Ranch, then returned to the fray. The combined force of federals caught up with the fleeing Confederates at Governor Connelly's ranch and captured a mountain howitzer and seven wagons that had been overlooked by Chivington. The First Cavalry squadron skirmished with the enemy at Albuquerque, and Canby's entire force was brought up for the last battle in the New Mexico campaign at Peralta. The cavalry tried all day to provoke a fight, but with little success. That night Sibley slipped away across the river to Los Lunas, and then started a long and disastrous march for El Paso. Canby followed down the Rio Grande valley, picking up scattered pieces of artillery and wagons until the Confederates had left only seven wagons of three hundred and twenty-seven they had started with.

So ended the New Mexican campaign, perhaps the most obscure in all American history. Yet in it had served three men somewhat known to fame, Canby, Chivington, and Kit Carson.

From Peralta Bernard had been sent to Fort Union to bring forward recruits that had arrived there. When he returned to Fort Union, he was assigned to command Company D, Captain Lord having been suspended following reports of the affair at the Pardes crossing and of his dilatoriness under Major Chivington. For a time the squadron of the First Cavalry, now greatly reduced, and a company of the Second Cavalry, manned the battery that had been commanded by McRae until he was killed at Valverde. In a short time, however, the squadron was returned to cavalry duty and was sent to Fort Union. Perhaps the impression has been given that Bernard was merely a fighter and of a low order of intelligence. This is not the case, although it is true that his educational advantages had been limited. But at this post he was appointed acting assistant quartermaster and assistant commissary of subsistence, tasks that required some facility in the keeping of accounts and were of some responsibility.

Meanwhile a war was going on far in the East—and it is hard for us to realize today just how far it was from Virginia to New Mexico in 1862. The regulars at Fort Union could have heard only intermittently and incompletely of the Peninsula campaign, of Antietam and of Fredericksburg, battles in which most of the First Cavalry was taking part. I can imagine Acting Lieutenant Bernard was not very happy over it. He had chalked up fifteen "fights and scrimmages" on his record, but No. 100 seemed far away while a year and a half of the Civil War was being wasted in idleness on a temporarily quiet

[41]

Indian frontier. He had learned much about horses and riding during his seven years of service. He had one of the finest horses at the post, and he spent much of his time riding, more often than not alone, for there were few officers at Fort Union and it was not often that more than one could be spared at a time.

One morning after troop drill Bernard rode off alone with no particular object in view save the pleasure of riding. He had not gone far when he jumped a gray fox. Of course he gave chase, not with any great expectation of doing anything about it. But both the fox and the horse seemed to enjoy it, and Bernard was quite willing to go along. Into arroyos, up hills, across gullies, through cactus and chaparral the chase led, but the smile on Reynard's face seemed a bit too supercilious for the officer's liking.

"All right, Mr. Fox, I'll just run you down, to show that a cavalryman and a real cavalry horse can do it!" he boasted, putting spurs to his mount. The horse seemed to enter into the spirit of the chase but Reynard put on more speed. For hours the chase continued, no one of the three having any disposition to quit. The fox was first to give way; he showed signs of weakening, and his pace slackened. Again Bernard touched spur to his horse's flank, and the cavalry animal responded instantly, pressing close on the heels of the quarry. Reynard tried to dodge around a clump of cactus, gave a leap into the air, gasped and fell dead.

Bernard reached down, picked up the fox, threw it over the pommel of his saddle, and rode slowly back to the fort. As he approached the post headquarters building he met the commanding officer who had just left his office. The colonel was astonished to see Bernard with a fox lying dead across his saddle and his horse a mass of foam.

"How did you get that fox, Lieutenant?" asked the commanding officer.

"I ran him down, sir," replied Bernard, at the same time reining in his horse and preparing to dismount.

"Hold on, there, hold on. Stay on that horse! Don't get off. I want to have the pleasure of handing you your first commission in the United States Army just as you are. Wait where you are."

While the commanding officer returned to his quarters, a number of officers and soldiers collected around Bernard, attracted by the unusual scene. The colonel returned and handed Bernard a paper.

"I want to hand you your commission as second lieutenant of Cavalry, Lieutenant Bernard, while you are mounted after running down and capturing with your bare hands a gray fox, a feat of which any cavalryman may be proud, however excellent he may be in the duties of a cavalryman. This commission arrived only an hour ago, perhaps at the very moment you captured the quarry."

Speed elsewhere was not so remarkable. Bernard had been appointed an acting second lieutenant January 5th; his commission in the grade was dated July 17th but it did not arrive until September 15th.

Meanwhile Captain Lord had demanded a court of inquiry on the charges for which he had been suspended. Bernard had no reason to spare Lord, for whom he had an accumulated contempt of several years standing. So you can imagine his, probably unexpressed, opinion when the court found as follows:

"The evidence given by Acting Second Lieutenant Bernard is that Captain Lord's command while proceeding to join Colonel Donaldson, had lost their guides, and were out of provisions, and that their horses were broken down, and that they were ignorant of the country, and they found themselves under the circumstances between two superior forces of the enemy. The court is of the opinion that the evidence places the conduct of Captain Lord in its true light, and exonerates him from all censure on that allegation."

Furthermore, in regard to charges involving Captain Lord's lack of enthusiasm during Major Chivington's campaign, the court found that Captain Lord had been ordered to charge a battery with his squadron, that the battery was actually charged by Captain Lord's command, and that he had led the charge.

And to add insult to injury, so far as Bernard was concerned, the court not only ordered that no further action be taken, but apologized to Captain Lord for the long delay in clearing him. Perhaps it did not occur to the lieutenant that the court of inquiry had paid him a very high compliment, for certainly if Captain Lord was justified in a surrender under the circumstances, Lieutenant Bernard should have been awarded a half dozen medals of honor for extricating the company "above and beyond the call of duty." Needless to say he didn't get them. Moreover Captain Lord, being restored to duty, was ordered to join the regiment in the East. The only consolation in this was that Bernard no longer was compelled to serve under Captain Lord's command.

While the Army of the Potomac was preparing for the spring offensive that was to result in the Chancellorsville and Gettysburg campaigns, Companies D and G of the First Cavalry were galloping one hundred and fifty-five miles to Camp Easton for an Indian hunting expedition along the Canadian River. The troops were ordered to remain at Camp Easton, but evidently were forgotten in the press of other business, and soon ran short of supplies.

Bernard volunteered to carry word of their plight to Fort Union and find out if anything more was expected of them along the Texas border. It was not fox chasing this time, but there were better reasons for the horse showing his heels, as wandering bands of Apache and Navajoes infested the region, and, in fact, Bernard was captured by one of these groups of Indians. But he had learned much of Indian ways during his eight years of service, and he was able to persuade them to let him go. He made the ride to Fort Union and back in record time and returned with good news. Orders had been received for the officers and noncommissioned officers to join the regiment in the East, where the companies would be reconstituted at full strength. The long exile was at an end.

Joyously the two troops returned to Fort Union. A few privates whose return to civilization was considered of little value to the Army of the Potomac were transferred to other units. The cadres remaining marched happily along the Raton trail to Fort Lyon, Fort Larned, Fort Riley, and Fort Leavenworth. There they took train behind a wheezy, wide-funneled, wood-burning locomotive to Carlisle Barracks, Pennsylvania, reaching there just after the invasion of that state had been ended by the battle of Gettysburg. Bernard's run of ill luck continued. He arrived too late for the battle, but was just in time for all the fun of mustering out nine-months' volunteers and emergency levies of militia called into service when General Robert E. Lee threatened to overrun the North. And Captain R. S. C. Lord of the First Cavalry had been brevetted major for gallant and meritorious service while Bernard's record read, "returned to Carlisle in August, and was on duty with Co. drilling and doing Garrison duty until October."

But in October, at last, came the long awaited order for Companies D and G, commanded by Second Lieutenant David Perry, to join the regiment at Camp Buford, Maryland.

IV

THE CIVIL WAR IN VIRGINIA*

LIEUTENANT PERRY reports Companies D and G, First Cavalry to the commanding officer, Camp Buford."

"Fine. Glad to see you, Lieutenant. I was just wondering where I would find a cavalry officer. Your regiment left for the front yesterday."

"My orders are to report to the regimental commander. Can we follow them?"

"Certainly, if your troops are mounted."

"But they're not. Where can we get horses?"

"Well, that's just it. I just had four hundred dismounted men sent in from the Cavalry Corps. Suppose you take charge of them and see what you can do about getting horses for them. Have you an officer I can appoint acting assistant quartermaster? Good. I'm sure you'll have no trouble, and will get away in a few days. Thank you, Lieutenant Perry. I'm glad to know some one will take charge of getting horses for the cavalrymen. Good day."

When this conversation was repeated to Lieutenant Bernard he hit the ceiling—if there was one. Of course he was the acting assistant quartermaster.

"Well, where do we get the horses?"

"Might try the quartermaster of the Cavalry Corps."

But there were no horses unassigned in charge of the Cavalry Corps. Bernard went to the quartermaster general of the Army of the Potomac. No horses.

---

*The incident of the encounter with Secretary Stanton is based upon an indication in Bernard's record. He did get the horses in the remarkably short time stated, and was assigned to command the detachment by order of the Secretary of War. "War of the Rebellion Records," Series I, Vol. 34, mentions Bernard's conduct at Todd's Tavern.

"Where do I go next?"

"Why, you'll get your horses as soon as we get them from the quartermaster general of the army. Your application will be placed on file and the requisition will be filled at the first opportunity."

"General, I rode half way from New Mexico to get into this war. If I'd known it was like this, I would have ridden all the way, and brought a herd with me. Surely somewhere this army owns a few horses."

"Well, you'll have to take that up with the quartermaster general. All the horses he has sent to the Army of the Potomac have been assigned."

And Bernard did take it up with the quartermaster general.

"Horses! Horses! Will the Army of the Potomac never get enough horses? And now you come bothering me for five or six hundred more. Why don't you ask the Secretary of War why he doesn't supply me with more money to buy horses?"

And Bernard did. Not in the least was this former blacksmith daunted by the whiskered fierceness and piercing eyes of Edwin M. Stanton.

"But why, young sir, do you come to me with your trivial demand for five hundred horses?" Stanton boomed. "Horses! What have I to do with horses? What do we have a quartermaster general for?—Who let this officer in?—Don't you know, sir, that there is a campaign on, that I have a thousand and one things to do; that there may be a battle today or tomorrow?"

"Yes, sir, and I have come from New Mexico to get into it. And now I am stopped because of a few damned horses. Not only for my own troops, but I've got to get four hundred more for a lot of men your Army of the Potomac can't take care of. We didn't ask some one else to take care of our men at Valverde and Apache Canyon and Glorietta. And your quartermaster general says there are not five hundred damned horses east of the Mississippi River."

"He does, does he? Secretary! Somebody! Here, you clerk! Write out an order that Lieutenant Bernard is to have—how many—five hundred and twenty horses. And right away, by order of the Secretary of War. And Clerk! Write out another order, assigning Lieutenant Bernard to command those four hundred skulkers. Where's that report from Buford? Add a paragraph—Lieutenant Bernard to take charge of those mules and wagons and whatever it is that never gets up to Buford. I believe this man'll get them there. Here are your orders, Lieutenant Bernard. Report your command to General Buford somewhere along Elk Run near Falmouth. Now get out of here. I have more important things to do than to get you horses and mules and wagons."

That Bernard had lost no time in slashing through this mass of red tape is shown by the fact that he had his detachment on the march before the end of the month and reported it to Major General John Buford, commanding the Reserve Brigade, First Division of the Cavalry Corps on October 30th. Buford was perhaps a bit perfunctory.

"So you've got here at last with the wagon train, Lieutenant?"

"Sir, I have been moving them as fast as I could ever since I was assigned to their command."

"No doubt, no doubt. It probably was no fault of yours that I have had to wait so long for them. And I believe you reported four hundred men. Have they had recruit drill?"

"Pardon me, sir, you perhaps misunderstood. These are the men you sent back for remount."

"Men I sent back! I sent no men back for remount except some a week or so ago."

"Yes, sir. They have been in my charge, and under Lieutenant Perry for a long time—perhaps ten days, sir."

"A long time—ten days! But they cannot have been remounted in that time. Not a quartermaster in the Army of the Potomac could have done it—or would have done it."

"They all have horses, sir, by order of the Secretary of War."

"I suppose so. The ways of the War Department and of Secretary Stanton are beyond the comprehension of the finite mind. But will you tell me why, after I had begged, implored, beseeched, demanded horses for my men, after I was told there were none and would be none, after I had sent men back as useless in the campaign because they were not mounted, then, before they have time to get on a ration return, they come trotting back, ready to go?"

"I do not know, sir, except that I asked Secretary Stanton for five hundred and twenty horses and he gave me an order for them."

"You asked Stanton for horses! And got them!"

"Yes, sir."

"Lieutenant Bernard, you are a man in a

"You asked Stanton for horses! And got them!"

thousand. Tell me what I can do for you."

"There is one thing you can do for me, general, that I would appreciate very much. If you can arrange to have some one take this detachment and this wagon train off my hands, I would like to report to my regiment, the First Cavalry."

And Bernard, having successfully upset a great war office, had little difficulty in getting untangled from the red tape of a brigade. Somewhere during his travels a commission dated June 21, 1863, had caught up with him, so it was as first lieutenant he reported to Captain Nelson B. Sweitzer, then commanding the regiment. Bernard was assigned to command Company I and six days later took part in his first skirmish in Virginia, at Culpeper.

Bernard's records, so far as they have been preserved, contain little detail of his services in the Virginia campaigns of the Civil War, and there is not space here to trace the history of the First Cavalry during this period. From November 9, 1863, to the end of the war he is credited with sixty-five battles, skirmishes, and engagements, a number that may seem excessive. But during the Civil War cavalry regiments took part in a very large number of actions, and in certain phases of the campaigns of 1864 and 1865 had almost daily combats, as will be seen in the following record of Bernard. It will be seen that on some occasions there was more than one fight on a single day.

BERNARD'S FIGHTS IN VIRGINIA
1863

November 5th, near Culpeper; 8th, Stevensburg; 26th, Mine Run.

1864

February 8th, Barnett's Ford.

March 10th, near Charlottesville; 11th, on Rapidan River.

May 6th, Todd's Tavern; 7th, Spotsylvania Courthouse; 10th, on the road to Beaver Dam; 10th, at Beaver Dam; 10th, on the road to Yellow Tavern; 11th, Yellow Tavern; 12th, at Meadow Bridge; 13th, after passing Meadow Bridge; 14th, Tunstall's Station; 15th, Tunstall's Station; 27th, while crossing Mattaponi River; 28th, Hawe's Shop; 30th, Old Church; 31st Cold Harbor (engagement).

June 1st, Cold Harbor (battle); 2d, Chickahominy River; 11th-12th Trevilian Station; 17th, White House Landing; 18th, Chickahominy River; 27th, Deep Bottom; 28th, Darby's Farm.

August 10th, Berryville; 10th, Stone Church; 11th, New Town; 12th, near Winchester; 13th, near Front Royal; 25th, Shepherdstown; 28th, Smithfield; 29th, Smithfield.

September 1st, near Halltown; 5th, Berryville; 15th, Opequan Creek; 19th, Winchester; 23d, Cedarville; 25th, Luray Valley; 26th, near Front Royal; 27th, in Luray Valley; 29th, near Staunton; 30th, Waynesboro.

December 22d, Rapidan River; 25th, Warrenton; 27th, Snicker's Gap.

1865

January 20th, Bunker's Hill.

March 3d, near Mount Jackson; 5th, near Staunton; 6th, Waynesboro; 12th, South Anna Bridge; 15th, White House Landing; 16th, on Chickahominy River; 29th, on road to Dinwiddie Courthouse; 30th, White Oak Road; 31st, at Dinwiddie Courthouse.

April 1st, Five Forks; 2d, Scott's Cross Roads; 4th, Drummond's Mills; 6th, Sailor's Creek; 7th, near Sailor's

Creek; 8th, near Appomattox Courthouse (night); 9th, Appomattox Courthouse.

Bernard, as first lieutenant, commanded Company I in the first considerable cavalry action of the 1864 campaign, that at Todd's Tavern, and for that fight he was brevetted captain for gallant and meritorious service. He was wounded, but evidently not seriously, as he took part in skirmishing at Spotsylvania the next day. The three fights of May 10th were in the hot pursuit of General J. E. B. Stuart, famous Confederate leader who was killed at the cavalry battle of Yellow Tavern the following day. At Hawe's Shop the cavalry adoped infantry tactics to drive the Confederates out of field fortifications, as a result of which the Cavalry Corps was able to push on and seize Cold Harbor, which was held May 31st with repeating carbines, almost as vicious a surprise weapon in that day as machine guns proved in the World War. This was one of the finest accomplishments of cavalry during the war, making full use of its mobility to seize an advance post, and then fight a dismounted action and withstand assault until the infantry arrived.

At Smithfield the First Cavalry performed one of its notable exploits. After two of its squadrons had been driven back, the reserve charged with saber in column of fours. It was opposed by a full brigade of the enemy using pistol. The Confederates halted to fire and the First Cavalrymen struck full tilt, sweeping the enemy to the rear. Bernard won his second brevet, that of major, at Smithfield, and ever afterwards had an appreciation of the usefulness of the saber. At Winchester September 19th the charge of the cavalry division under Major General Wesley Merritt was decisive in the victory. The First and Second Cavalry regiments captured two stands of colors and two hundred prisoners, the First suffering thirty-seven

Making full use of its mobility to seize an advance post and then fight a dismounted action.

casualties. Bernard found himself temporarily in command of the regiment during Brigadier General Alfred T. A. Torbert's raid tô Gordonsville in December, an indication of how heavy casualties had been among officers of the regiment, for Bernard was a junior first lieutenant.

Almost daily skirmishing during the first nine days of April brought the war to an end with Lee's surrender. Presumably Bernard had enjoyed it. As a final reward he was given a double brevet, as lieutenant colonel and colonel, dated March 13, 1865 "for gallant and meritorious service during the war." Thus he was entitled to be addressed as "Colonel Bernard" although his actual rank, and, more important, his pay, was that of a first lieutenant. But even that was a considerable advance over the rank of blacksmith, a trade that represented not only his beginning in the army, but also his highest attainment in civil life. There is no evidence that he contemplated leaving the army.

Bernard had missed one important battle during his tour of service in Virginia, and it probably was the only battle he did not regret missing. While Cedar Creek was being fought, with Sheridan twenty miles away, Lieutenant Bernard was at an even greater distance for he was on twenty days' sick leave. Now girls of the Civil War period were not greatly different from those of 1917 and 1918 in their desire to "do their bit," and among those who tried to cheer the sick and wounded was a little fifteen-year-old Washington girl, Alice Virginia Frank. When Alice found that this black-bearded lieutenant had actually fought Indians in the far west before the war, she thought of him as a sort of modern incarnation of Captain John Smith and Daniel Boone, which he was, more or less. Lieutenant Bernard had never had much time to talk to pretty little girls about his adventures, and

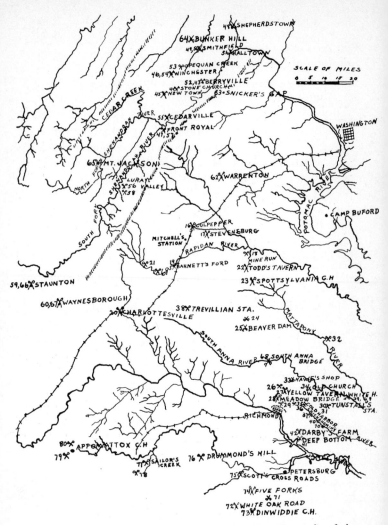

*A part of Virginia, showing locations of Bernard's fights
Numbers 16 to 80 inclusive*

(Based on maps in the Personal Memoirs of General Phil H.
Sheridan and other contemporary sources.)

it was an unusual experience to find one who was interested in hearing about such things. Now add to this the self-evident fact that hunting up a dozen battles a month does not leave much time for social diversion in the Virginia of 1864, and you will not be particularly surprised that this young man of thirty-two years should be interested in a girl who paid some attention to him, even if she were only fifteen. And it must be emphasized that the age was a leisurely one, and a man might occasionally wait for his future wife to grow up. One might cite a conspicuous example in George E. Pickett, leader of the Confederate charge at Gettysburg, who is said to have chosen his future bride when she was only five years old, and he already a graduate of West Point.

Be that as it may, Bernard did not prolong his illness on Alice's account. He was in the field again four days after the battle of Cedar Creek. But now that the war was over, and the regiment had marched back from Appomattox to Petersburg, the Virginia town that had been besieged for so long a time by the Army of the Potomac, Bernard took six days' leave, and I think we may be reasonably certain that Alice heard some more war stories. His stay was somewhat lengthened by the fact that the regiment, meanwhile, was moved to Alexandria to take part in the "Grand Review" of the Army of the Potomac at the capital. Immediately after this parade the First Cavalry was sent to New Orleans.

Service in the south after the war had little appeal for regular army officers generally, and none at all for Bernard. It was in no very cheerful frame of mind, then, that he brought his company to regimental headquarters. It made him no happier to learn that Captain Lord was in command of the regiment. So it was in quite formal tones he announced:

"Lieutenant Bernard reports Company I to the commanding officer."

"So you still command the company, Lieutenant Bernard. Too bad Captain Baker cannot join us." Lord may have meant the remark innocently, but it was not so taken.

"And I think it highly unfortunate that we cannot have some or one of our field officers present, sir."

"If you intend anything personal by your remark, Lieutenant, I think I have sufficient rank to command a regiment. I am a lieutenant colonel, by brevet. And I have commanded the regiment on the field of battle, for that matter."

"And if you mean anything personal by your remark, I am a colonel, by brevet, I have also commanded the regiment in action, and moreover, I have never commanded even a detachment that tried to dodge a fight."

"Lieutenant Bernard, your language is disrespectful toward your commanding officer."

"Captain Lord, I have no respect for you as commanding officer."

"Report to your quarters in arrest, sir."

The court martial was of the opinion that this quarrel was a rather childish affair. Officially it sentenced Bernard to be reprimanded by the departmental commander for insubordinate conduct. Unofficially its judge advocate expressed himself to Bernard as follows:

"Bernard, you take your courage so much for granted that it doesn't occur to you that anyone else should be less audacious than you. It still irks you that a court of inquiry cleared Captain Lord of the charges you brought against him, and it has never occurred to you that their finding was one of the finest tributes to your leadership ever put on official record. Since then Captain Lord has won brevets for his courage at Gettysburg and at Five Forks and they were both deserved and there has been no criticism of his conduct on other fields."

"I suppose you are right. But it does seem that I will never get through serving under Captain Lord."

But he did, for this was the last time. Afterward he was glad that they had made up their quarrel, for only a year later Lord died.

In September Bernard was given two months' leave of absence, and for the first time since the beginning of the war visited his old home in Tennessee. He also went to Washington, and this time he and Alice became engaged, with the understanding that they should not marry for another year.

On his return to New Orleans he was pleased to learn that the regiment had been ordered to the far west. Under command of Major Albert G. Brackett, a pioneer cavalry historian, the regiment sailed for San Francisco in the last days of 1865. The reassembling of a regiment after the Civil War was a slow process. In California Captain E. M. Baker arrived to take charge of his company. Bernard, as first lieutenant, had commanded it nearly three years. In March Company I left the Presidio of San Francisco for Fort Vancouver.

From Camp Watson, Oregon, in May, Lieutenant Bernard led forty-five men of Company I to his first Indian campaign after the Civil War. It was not a very important affair—a small band of Snake Indians had caused some trouble and Bernard's troopers were ordered to "pursue and punish." But he was warmly commended in regimental orders for his promptitude and energy in marching six hundred and thirty miles in twenty-six days, during which the hostiles were defeated three times. Bernard himself was present at only one of these, but it is to be noted that the men trained by him soon became permeated with his ideas. Thus Sergeant Thomas W. Connor with nineteen men attacked an Indian camp on Rattlesnake Creek and utterly routed a force of eighty warriors. The scene of this expedition was Crooked River, Silver Creek, Harney Lake, Malheur Lake, the Owyhee country and the headwaters of Malheur River; its results, thirteen Indians killed, nine horses, two mules and a number of prisoners taken—the indefiniteness in prisoners is no doubt due to the difficulty of distinguishing between captives and guests—and the camps of the Indians destroyed. And it was noted that the conduct of the operation "furnishes an example well worthy of imitation."

So much for that. Indian wars and reconstruction policies in the South resulted in large increases in the army. July 28th Bernard received his captaincy. Three years later the army was sharply reduced, leaving a large surplus of officers. Bernard's captaincy lasted a long time. In August he was ordered to the recruiting service at Carlisle Barracks, Pennsylvania, but if he had expected to see Alice on this trip east he was disappointed, for the day after his arrival he was ordered to conduct three hundred and fifty recruits to San Francisco by way of Panama. He made a fourth coast-to-coast trip in one year—something of a record for that period—and returned to Carlisle in November.

Captain Bernard was married to Alice Frank at Washington, December 6, 1866. She lacked three months of being eighteen years of age. All too soon she was to learn of the trials and vicissitudes of an army bride. At first they lived at Carlisle Barracks. Perhaps she complained when Captain Bernard was sent with parties of recruits to New Orleans, Nashville, Montgomery and Fort Leaven-

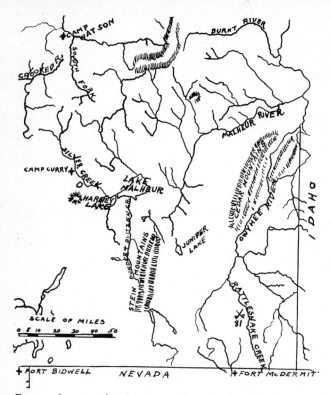

Eastern Oregon, showing scene of Bernard's campaign against the Snake Indians and the location of his 81st fight.

(Based on Keeler's Map of the United States west of the Mississippi River and other contemporary sources.)

worth. There were to come many times when she would wish that he would be sent to no places more inaccessible. She could be thankful that he was with her when their first child, Harry Edwin Bernard, was born December 23, 1867.

The following August she was to learn much more

about the life of an army wife. With one hundred and fifty recruits they went to New York City, where they were joined by Colonel G. A. H. Blake, commanding officer of the First Cavalry. From there they sailed for Panama and San Francisco. For a short time Captain Bernard commanded a camp of recruits at Angel Island, but his next duty was to take a party to the companies of the regiment in Arizona. Then troubles began. Smallpox broke out among the recruits and they were landed at Drum Barracks. They were hustled out to an isolation camp at Domingues Ranch to remain until all traces of the disease disappeared. When the quarantine was lifted, Bernard speeded for Fort Yuma, California, arriving just in time for the birth of his first daughter, Fannie Eugenia, October 27th. The baby was only a few weeks old when the family started for Tucson, Arizona, for it was high time that the captain should assume command of his company. You would think that after all this Alice would deserve some few days' domestic peace, and she had them, to the number of six. Then the captain was sent into Mexico to purchase pack mules, being gone from December 8th to January 29th. January 30th he was home—if it can be called that. The next day he took his company on an expedition against the Arivaipa Apaches.

V

COCHISE AND THE APACHES*

A SQUAW had arrived at Camp Grant with information to the effect that the Arivaipas wanted to make peace. The real story was that this squaw had had a little domestic difficulty as a result of which her husband had threatened to beat her and kill her child. Under these conditions—for an Apache husband was quite capable of carrying out such threats—she decided to place herself under the protecting aegis of the First Cavalry, and in order to be sure of winning favor among new friends, concocted the story of the peace message. She was taken along as guide for the expedition which consisted of thirty-eight men and two officers of Bernard's Company G, twenty-four men and one officer of Company K, seven Indian scouts, four packers and sixteen pack mules.

Leaving the pack train behind, Bernard pushed into the Arivaipa Mountains, finding two abandoned rancherias or camps, but no Apaches. Picking up the pack train, he crossed the mountain "through as hard a snow storm as I ever saw in my life in any country" but without finding any sign of Arivaipas. He then sent Lieutenant A. H. Stanton with all except twenty-seven men back along the trail as a decoy, while he himself led and guided the small force remaining through snow fifteen to twenty inches deep in a circuitous route to the highest point of the range. Note that Bernard did the guiding; his Indian scouts had long since given up the idea. His system? It was much simpler than that usually described in the books of western adventure. He merely moved "to-

---

History of Arizona, by T. E. Farish, Vol. VIII, Chapter II, for Chiricahua Pass.

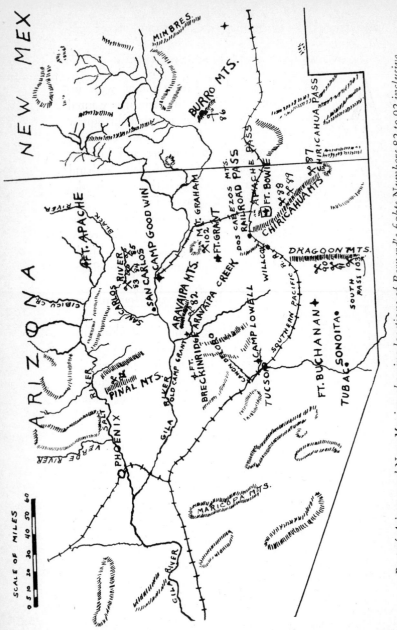

Part of Arizona and New Mexico, showing locations of Bernard's fights Numbers 82 to 92 inclusive
(Based on map of Arizona Territory by Lieutenant F. A. Smith, 1879, and other contemporary sources.)

wards the points where there was most certainty of finding Indians or Indian signs." Indian signs? Again ele-
mentary, Dr. Watson. "I saw a smoke issuing from
under the rock. Looking further up the mountain to my
left I saw thirty or forty Indians in full retreat up the
mountain. I ordered the charge."

Now you see how simple it all is. Strange that so
many other expeditions failed to find Apaches, even when
the snow was not the worst seen in any country. Of
course, even primer students in the annals of the west
know that the cavalry charge ends the show. Let us see.

"Every man did his best to reach the fleeing Indians,
but cavalry mounted as my company is, upon poor
mustangs and broken down stage horses, can do little in
pursuing Indians up a snow-covered mountain." What's
this? Broken down stage horses? And in an official report,
too, that might even get to the Secretary of War; certainly did get to Brevet Major General E. O. C. Ord, commanding the Department of California. No wonder Bernard never knew upon returning from an expedition
whether he would be recommended for another brevet or
hauled before another court martial.

But the pursuit continued up the mountain, "where we
run into another rancheria; here eight Indians were killed
and six prisoners (women and children) were captured.
The Indians lost all their camp equipage"—that would
have sounded very well in the official report had this
honest captain not gone on to say—"which was very
little. The only things of any value captured were three
bows and some arrows, a few buckskins, butcher knives,
awls, and a few baskets." Yet their captain, Chiquito,
did not want peace.

A very little affair, of no importance whatsoever. "One
man of Company G while attempting to run his horse by

others on his front, lost his footing; both horse and rider rolled down the mountain about two hundred feet; both were badly bruised, but not seriously injured." That was important to him, no doubt, for two hundred feet at least. "Had I remained out five days longer I would have lost half my horses." But then, of course, they were only broken down stage horses. "Private Elijah Peck captured two women and children. . . . One little boy that was captured is the brother of one of our Indian scouts. His father and mother were both killed, and I gave him to his brother (who is an enlisted Indian) to raise. Another small boy is in the hands of Colonel Ilges.* He has neither father nor mother. Colonel Ilges desires to retain the boy and provide for him. They are too small to care for themselves. The remaining children are with their mothers, who are captives. . . . They all say that they do not want to go back to their tribes, and I believe they would not go if released, for their appearance indicates that they have been nearly starved." A brutal sort of warfare, where colonels and privates take infant prisoners to raise. But a very minor affair—

"Returned to post February 9, 1869, having marched 250 miles. Continued on duty in command of post and company until March 1, 1869." So long a time that the official records make particular note of it. Perhaps not so long to Alice.

Again Brevet Colonel Bernard commanded, and since his men customarily called him "colonel" we may as well begin the practice, always remembering that he actually was a captain commanding a company and drew a captain's pay. This time he had twenty-eight men of his own company and a lieutenant and ten men of Company

*Brevet Lieutenant Colonel Guido Ilges (Captain, 14th Infantry).

[66]

E, Thirty-second Infantry, mounted and equipped as cavalry, fourteen Indian scouts, six Mexican packers, a guide with the euphonic name of Merigilao Grigallo, and, as Medical Corps detachment, George Campbell, hospital steward. They marched along the Dragoon Mountains and the Chiricahua Mountains to Camp Bowie, one hundred and sixty-five miles, then along the Dos Cabezos Mountains, across Railroad Pass (still minus the railroad) and Mount Graham to the Goodwin Road and Camp Goodwin, one hundred and twenty-three miles. Results so far: one Indian trail leading south. Then down the Gila River, to the eastern branch of the San Carlos with perpendicular banks some six hundred feet deep. Upon descending into this canyon in an attempt to cross it, the entire command was caught in a heavy rain during which the water rose so rapidly that only a rapid scramble up the steep banks saved the whole outfit from drowning. But all this is mere incident of nineteen days' scouting to small effect.

On March 19th luck changed. First a camp of nine huts was taken and destroyed. Its occupants had fled. Then two Indian women were captured—one was found in a hole of water, all covered with the exception of her face. These two guided the expedition to a camp of thirty-seven huts. "A charge was made"—but ever Colonel Bernard must be prosaic—"with little success, more than to do considerable shooting." How sadly he needed a press agent. Two children and two burros were captured. But the day was not over. The woman prisoners led the expedition to a third camp, one of fifty-nine huts. But lest you think that this woman who had buried herself to the nose in water to escape had succumbed to a sudden excess of admiration for the flag, be it noted that "the camp was in a very deep canon, at the foot of some

[67]

high hills, the command being exposed to their view about a mile before reaching the camp, by going the way the women had taken us. The Indians commenced to run away as soon as they saw us. The charge was ordered, but when we reached the camp we had to do all our shooting at long range, and through thick bushes."

But if no great numbers of Indians were killed, the fight was not without results. Bernard estimated the supplies captured as weighing twenty-five tons. Perhaps you would be interested in knowing what sort of taxable property is to be found in an Apache rancheria of 1869. Here it is: at least a ton of mescal, many bushels of roots, greens, seeds, nuts and other edibles, axes, hatchets, hoes, baskets, kettles, knives, bows and arrows, canteens, skins, lariats, moccasins, manta blankets, paints, medicines, charms and needles. The owners of this plunder are described as of the tribe of Babet-el-cha, which sounds more Arabic than it does Arizonian.

You may sometimes see it stated that the Apaches carried on little agriculture and will wonder at the hoes and other evidences of farming. Bernard says in this report, "I have seen fields of corn on the Gila, San Carlos, Bonito, Prieta and other streams around the Pinal and White Mountains, equal to any raised in this country." And he comes to the very sensible conclusion that "if a reservation were given to these Indians sufficiently large for them to hunt, plant, and burn mescal in, that they would remain at peace," which sort of idea was very common among army officers, but somehow never seemed to meet government favor for any considerable time. You wonder why? There was profit for some one in trying to keep the Indians "upon six miles square of sage brush desert, as the Goodwin reservation is." Why waste good land on Indians when some American might make use of it! Of course the American settler, his wife and children might be tortured to death by the dispossessed Apache, but that was of minor interest to another American settler who might have cattle or other supplies to sell for distribution as Indian rations. It was against the interest of a large portion of the pioneer population for the Indian to be self-supporting, and that was one of the primary reasons why the pioneers suffered so much from the Indians. Even so, the rationing system might have worked out, had the Indians actually obtained any considerable proportion of what was allotted to them.

"These Indians need some person who is firm and who can give them what he promises." So says Bernard, and you will see that he was not merely an Indian fighter. For lack of a firm policy, rigidly enforced, both the soldier and the settler suffered. After others had stirred up the mischief, it was Bernard's duty to "pursue and punish." Very ably he did his duty.

After the capture of the third rancheria, Bernard's next interest was his pack train. His expedition had campaigned five days on three days' rations, hard marches by day and night through rain and over snow, with guard duty every other night. The pack train was found stranded across the Gila River, having insufficient force with it to effect a crossing in the stage of high water that had been reached. So Bernard put his men to building rafts on which they crossed and returned to Camp Goodwin, completing a march of four hundred and thirty-one miles March 22d. After several days' rest, he marched his command to Camp Grant. There he was met by an alarming message from Tucson. Baby Fannie was ill. Hastily he turned over his command to Major John Green, mounted a fresh horse, and started for Tucson, a distance of sixty-five miles by air line. It was a wild dash over mountain trail by pass and canyon. He arrived a few hours before Baby Fannie died, March 30th. It was a heavy blow. He had been on field duty so much of the time during the five months and three days of this baby's life he had seen very little of her. He could find some assuagement of his grief in active duty, but the days must have been lonesome ones for Alice. Always a very quiet person—an enlisted man who served several years in Bernard's company cannot remember ever hearing her voice —she was devoted to her family and her life was her ever-shifting home.

Bernard's first expedition after this tragedy was a sadly unsuccessful one. There came to Camp Lowell at Tucson a report that a wagon train had been attacked in the Canyon del Oro by a band of Pinal Indians. Colonel Bernard's troop was sent to the rescue. In motion pictures the cavalry always arrives in the nick of time, but in the real life of the West it did not always turn out that way. Bernard's troop arrived too late; the wagon train had been captured. For two days, without rations, his men pursued the marauders, but with no success.

Shortly after this dash, Company G was ordered to Camp Bowie and Colonel Bernard assumed command of that post May 29, 1869. It was familiar territory, and for the rest of the year he campaigned against an old enemy, Cochise, at this period the most famous of Apache chiefs. In a report of this period Bernard gives his version of the Apache Pass affair and his opinion of Cochise—although he spells it Coches and sometimes Cocheis—in a paragraph:

"All they know of whites is their evil deeds," he starts out. "One of the worst Indians now on this continent is Coches. This Indian was always at peace with the whites until 1860, when he and his family were invited to dine with an officer of the Army, who had his company ready to arrest him for the purpose of keeping him as a hostage for the return of a boy stolen by the Pinals. Since that time this Indian has burned alive thirteen white men that I know of, besides most cruelly torturing to death, by cutting small pieces out of them, five others; fifteen others I know by putting lariats around their necks, tied their hands behind them, and dragged them to death. All this was done in the spring of 1860, within twenty miles of where Camp Bowie now stands. This Indian was at peace until betrayed and wounded by white men. He now, when spoken to about peace, points to his scars and says, 'I was at peace with the whites until they tried to kill me for what other Indians did; I now live and die at war with them.'"

Bernard's troop scouted in the direction of Mount Graham June 6th to 10th, 1869. He started out again from Camp Bowie June 26th, this time to the Burro Mountains, where the troop celebrated the Fourth of July by fighting its first battle with Cochise's band. August 8th to 12th it made the first of a series of scouts into the Chiricahua Mountains, Cochise's stronghold.

By this time Company G was well mounted, due to its captain's constant insistence on this point. "If my men had been mounted on good horses, or even on bad cavalry horses, I could have killed or captured many of the Indians," he said of his March expedition, "but many of my horses are over fifteen years of age, others wild and unmanageable, and all very wild, poor and unfit for cavalry service, being without exception broken down and worthless."

But in October Lieutenant W. H. Winters reported he was "hot upon the trail" of Cochise's band running off a herd of cattle and Bernard was proud to report that "I was only seven hours in making the distance (forty-five miles) from this post to the point where I met Lieut. Winters," returning with the cattle, "and had the despatch been delivered at the post in proper time, I should have just about reached the scene of action at the time Lieut. Winters did.

"The horses my troop is now mounted on enable the men to do their duty as cavalrymen should. With such horses, and with such an officer as Lieutenant Winters to move the troop, they will invariably meet with success." You may think this is rubbing it in, but he is not through yet. "Had the troop been mounted as they have been for the last two years Coches would again have been successful, and have reached his home in Chihuahua, or New Mexico, with all his plunder. As it is,—" because we have some horses, of course, "he lost it all, with some of his own stock and 12 of his warriors killed, and doubtless many more wounded."

Brevet Brigadier General Thomas C. Devin, commanding the sub-district of southern Arizona, immediately ordered reinforcements to Colonel Bernard, but without waiting for them Bernard was off again on the trail within eight days with two troops, G of the First Cavalry and G of the Eighth Cavalry, a total force of sixty-one men. He marched only at night as far as the scene of Lieutenant Winters' fight, but was unable to pick up the trail there in the dark. If he had had a few fictional Indian scouts with him, able to follow the slightest trail on the darkest night that ever was, he might have been more successful, but unfortunately there were real live Indian scouts, with no motion picture experience, and he had to wait until daylight. The next morning the trail was easily followed to an abandoned Indian camp on a mountain side. Ned Buntline and the other heroes of Beadle's

[72]

Dime Library were still absent and it took about two hours to pick up the trail from this point. Then it was found, not by one of the keen-nosed Indians nor by one of the self-reputationed "scouts of the prairie," but by Colonel Bernard himself, "who could see a clearly defined trail, just as you or I could," in the words of one of his former enlisted men, and in addition "knew Indians and could make excellent guess as to their location when he wished to find them." It is notable that it was Colonel Bernard quite often who found the trail.

After about ten miles he noticed a fresh track running in the same direction his force was moving. He knew this was of a hostile scout and that the main body must be near by, so ordered a gallop. In about five minutes he came upon a camp, evidently abandoned a day or two before. Here, of course, the trail was lost again, so Bernard halted his command while he went in one direction to find it, sending the guide in another. Neither had any success, but went out again. This time he sent five men with the guide to go to the top of a rocky mesa. Bernard had gone about two hundred yards into a canyon when he turned to see how the men were getting on, and noticed several Indians running ahead of them. He dashed back at high speed, ordered his men to tie their horses to trees and get up the slope as fast as possible, leaving six men to watch the horses. Before the command had got half way up the hill, the Apaches opened fire on the guide and the five men with him. The six dropped to shelter behind rocks. Immediately firing commenced from all parts of the slope. The troopers rushed forward to a ledge about thirty yards from the Apaches, but in this charge Sergeant Stephen S. Fuller of the Eighth Cavalry and Private Thomas Collins of the First were killed and Private Edwin Elwood of the Eighth wounded, all with rifle

Ordered to occupy the hilltop.

balls, although most of the Indians were using arrows. The men dug in and for a half hour continued a careful picking off of every Indian who exposed himself. But Bernard did not expect to accomplish anything by trench warfare, so he turned over command at this point to Lieutenant John Lafferty of the Eighth and went back to dispose of the rear guard and pack train.

Bernard had a very high respect for the generalship of Cochise. "He is one of the most intelligent hostile Indians on this continent," was his official expression. The position occupied by Cochise's band was admirably situated for defense. It was on a level table land, or mesa, rising about six hundred yards from the bottom of Chiricahua Pass. Its crest was bounded by a precipice ranging from five to twenty feet high; in its rear was the principal slope of the mountain, very high and rocky, and on each side was a deep rocky canyon. Loose rocks and many oak trees were of advantage to both sides.

A survey of the situation soon showed that no advance could be made from the present line without running up against another precipice. Accordingly Lafferty was ordered to fall back to a small flat, thickly covered with timber. Cochise's band was well armed, and heavy volleys were fired whenever a soldier exposed himself, so the withdrawal had to be made by dashing from rock to rock. It was found impossible to bring in the bodies of the two dead. As it was, Private Charles H. Ward of the First fell over the rocks in dashing down the hill and broke his leg.

Bernard's first concern, of course, was to get the two wounded men to a place of safety; his next, as you might expect, was his horses—no broken down stage horses, these—for they were under fire in the place where they had been corralled. When these, and the pack train, had been taken to the rear, Bernard took twenty men and moved to the right, hoping to get in the rear of Cochise, but whenever one of his men was seen to be within range, the Apaches opened fire. Bernard gave up the right, but hoped the left was less well guarded, or that he could get in position for a charge across it. He took thirty mounted men on a wide flanking move around a hill, but as he approached the mesa he discovered the ravine that protected it on that side, and before he could lead his horses down into and out of the ravine, Cochise's tribesmen opened fire. First Sergeant Francis Oliver was then given fifteen men and ordered to occupy the hilltop, where he and his men were able to pick off several Indians. The object now was to recover the bodies, and Bernard ordered his second lieutenant, Brevet Captain John Q. Adams to join Lieutenant Lafferty with all the men that could be spared in a charge for this purpose, but just as Adams reached the front line, Lafferty was hit in the face and by the time he had been taken to the rear it was sunset, and too late to effect anything.

Bernard now very sensibly withdrew his entire force. He was willing to give the field to Cochise in the hope that the Apache would consider it a victory and give up his strong position. Bernard's men had killed eighteen of the enemy; two troopers had been killed. He made no estimate of the enemy wounded, but was sure it was a large number. With some sixty men Bernard had inflicted upon a hundred or two hundred Apaches the severest punishment ever suffered by Cochise, which is something when it is considered that the wily Chiricahua chief had usually eluded all forces sent out against him.

For this fight Bernard was recommended for a brevet of brigadier general, Lafferty and Adams were recommended for brevets of major and thirty-one enlisted men for medals of honor.

Bernard brought his wounded into the post, and four days later, October 24th, started out again with the same two troops, reinforced by eight Indian scouts. He found the Apaches gone from Chiricahua Pass and was able to bury his dead. While this was being done, scouts reported seeing horses in a nearby canyon, presumably left there as a decoy into an ambush. The next morning Bernard took his troops into this canyon, leaving Lieutenant Winters in rear with the pack train. Soon Indians were seen running high up the mountain trying to gain Bernard's rear. His flanking scouts opened fire on them, and soon Winter's men opened up. The Apaches were driven to the top of a mountain where they could not be reached, so Bernard went into camp. By this time they were ready for peace talk, and during the night they conferred with Bernard's Indian scouts under a flag of truce. But he would grant no terms save unconditional surrender.

Meanwhile Bernard had sent word back to Camp Bowie that he had found Cochise's band again and requested that any cavalry reinforcements that had arrived be sent forward. The cavalry had not reported yet, but Capt. T. S. Dunn did not want to be left out of a fight, so stripped the post of every available man and marched forth with nineteen infantrymen, making fifty miles in twenty hours with the hope of being of assistance. This was too small a force to do any good, so the bold captain consented to return to the dangerously denuded post with an escort of six cavalrymen, leaving his infantrymen. The next day Captain Harrison Moulton arrived with Company C of the First Cavalry, thirty-one men, bringing Bernard's total force to one hundred and eighteen.

Bernard marched up the mountain October 30th to find it deserted. He moved down the mountain into the canyon, where some horses were seen. Cochise's Apaches opened fire on the troops as soon as they reached the low ground; the fire was returned and two Indians were killed. Lieutenant Winters with the infantry and Eighth Cavalry troop was covering the descent and he was able, with rifle fire, to keep the Apaches so far up the opposite mountain that they could do no effective shooting, so Cochise's men were reduced to rolling huge stones down on their opponents. But this was effective in stopping further advance. A flanking operation would only have driven them to another mountain, and the soldiers were very tired. So Bernard gave it up, and returned to Camp Bowie. There Captain John Barry had arrived with Company L of the First Cavalry, thirty infantrymen, and twenty-one Mexican cavalrymen with an officer, who had come across the line to help in the Cochise round-up. Captain Barry with the troopers and Mexicans was sent out on November 2d and Bernard followed the next day, joining Barry by midnight. The combined force now numbered one hundred and fifty-six.

By this time Cochise was worried. His Apaches had gone to the trouble of constructing a road through the mountains to move their stock out, and this monumental labor on the part of Apaches proves they were worried. Only one Indian was seen and he was killed. On him was found a breech-loading rifle that had been taken from a mail escort in an Apache raid.

Colonel Bernard pushed his pursuit so rapidly that Cochise gave up all plans for resistance and scattered his band. This is the usual end of an Apache chase and there was nothing more to do. Somewhere, sometime, Cochise's band would reassemble, and then the troops would have another chance. It was not practicable to chase individual Indians through the mountains. In summing up the results of the campaign, Bernard counted thirty-three Indians killed, an indefinite number wounded, twenty horses and mules captured.

"This wily Indian, Coches, will not stand to fight a command as large as mine was, and perhaps will never again give battle to any number of troops under circumstances so favorable to himself as he did on the 20th of October on the rocky mesa," he predicted. So the command was returned to Camp Bowie and the visiting companies dismissed.

In January, Bernard started out again on Cochise's trail with his two original Companies G, surprised the Indians on January 27th, killed thirteen and captured two of them, and took thirteen horses, a mule and a burro. The next day he had a second skirmish in the Dragoon Mountains, and captured and destroyed Cochise's camp. Cochise was now near the end of his career. Major General O. O. Howard, pious but supremely courageous, persuaded T. J. Jeffords, scout and mail coach official, to take him to Cochise. Alone, the general stayed in the Apache camp until he had made a permanent peace. Eventually the old Chiricahua chieftain died at peace with the world.

From February until December of 1870, Bernard also was at peace with the world, at Camp Bowie, a period of quiet that Alice no doubt appreciated. In April Kate May was born. She lived to become the wife of General Beaumont B. Buck who survives her.

But there were other Apaches. On December 21st, Bernard started on a four hundred and fifty mile expedition against the Pinal Apaches, having slight skirmishes with them December 27th and 28th and capturing their camp in the Pinal Mountains on the first day of

January, 1871. Nine Indians were killed in this engagement, and twenty-three head of stock captured.

In February the company marched out from Camp Bowie on foot for a change of station, walking three hundred and three miles to Tucson, Yuma, and San Diego, and from there by steamer to Benicia Barracks. From there Bernard went to Camp Bidwell, California, where he remained until December 4, 1872, a long and peaceful period broken only by the successful pursuit of a deserter to Virginia City, Nevada. During this year his son John Jay Bernard was born, in April. John was killed in Cuba during the Spanish-American war.

VI
BERNARD'S TROOP

BY this time Bernard's troop was becoming a crack outfit—in the field. "Unless mounted, the troop did not shine in garrison life," says one competent observer. "They were never beauties in the field, unless engaged in a hot fight. Then they became a real unit, showing the effects of the training Bernard, whose chief demands were that his men should ride, shoot, handle the saber, and not get drunk too frequently. Of course we had some failures who never could be made to fit in. These usually deserted, thus keeping the troop fairly well cleaned up." Even a first sergeant might carry out this idea of "natural selection," for "Black Jack" Raymond was among those who departed for points unknown.

It was a crack troop, but, as these remarks will indicate, by no means a picked troop. In these days since the World War and the Great Depression the army has become a somewhat exclusive educational institution, with waiting lists of candidates maintained at recruiting stations, where qualifications are carefully scrutinized and the fortunate recruits who are selected consider a "hitch" in the army the next best thing to a college degree. But in the years after the Civil War the principal course of study was offered in the School of Indian Fighting and the chief requirements of recruits were that they be able to walk many miles on an empty stomach and preserve the hair on top of their heads as long as possible. Recruiting officers took the best material they could find, of course, but the regular army was not very popular in some localities, and the candidates were usually none too numerous. Of course a few adventurous youths from good families were attracted by the lure of the then lurid Wild West and an occasional college graduate might be found in the ranks. The popularity of Irish and German comedians in the period has brought about a more widespread introduction of characters of these two nationalities into the literature of the army in the west than the actual number of immigrants with the colors would probably justify. There were, of course, many Irish and German soldiers, and some few of scattering nationalities. At the bottom of the list was a sprinkling of those who had left the more populous centers of the east to promote, by their absence, the general welfare of those communities, no doubt much to the relief of the police and other local authorities. These characters usually did not stay long. There were occasional cases of men who enlisted solely for transportation to the land of promise, promptly deserting on arrival. But this element can easily be exaggerated. Stories and plays of the period had to have villains, and fictional villains were probably commoner than those in real life.

The great majority of soldiers in the ranks were just average Americans—boys from farms and villages and cities, out to see the world, anxious for adventure, envious of their elder brothers who had yarns to tell of the Civil War. Many of them grew old in the service, a little disillusioned perhaps, complaining about little things, just as the soldiers of Joshua, of Caesar, of the Black Prince, of Napoleon and of Pershing grumbled, but meaning little by it. But take them all-in-all, as one meets them here and there, these Indian fighters were just about average men and perhaps a little better in quality than would be supposed off hand. Their diaries show about the same sort of reactions to similar circumstances as are to be found in diaries of citizen-soldiers of the World War, and the veteran of that conflict, or the soldier of today, would probably find himself quite at home in Fort Bidwell in 1875 once he had become accustomed to the somewhat less comfortable uniform and the lack of a great many modern gadgets.

This was the sort of material Bernard had to work with, and there seems little doubt that if he could not make soldiers of them, it was of little use for anyone else to try. The experience of one recruit, Private Charles B. Hardin, who joined the troop just before the Modoc War, will give some idea of Bernard's ways.

"My great admiration for Colonel Bernard had its beginning within five minutes after I first saw him," says Hardin. "We arrived at his post, Fort Bidwell, California, on or about October 27, 1872, after a hard march, dismounted, from Reno, Nevada. I was but a lad, under eighteen years of age, and the last two days of marching with a high fever, had about done me up. Upon arrival we were lined up for inspection by Colonel Bernard. I was scarcely able to stand, and could not have stood but for having been braced up by the men on either side of me. My heart sank when I saw this, to me, fierce-looking captain approaching. I felt sure that he would think me drunk, and treat me accordingly. I had just been through the cavalry recruit depot where all so-called discipline had been in the hands of hard-boiled sergeants and kindness was taboo. Was I to be cursed, possibly knocked down, and ordered to the guard house? I was honestly scared.

"This big, black-bearded captain stopped in front of me and gazed at me for a moment, while my heart fluttered. Then, turning to the first sergeant, he said:

" 'This man is sick. See that he is cared for at once.'

"He had but done his plain duty, but he had gained an admirer who ever afterward was ready to go the limit

[83]

for him. I was to be safe under this man. It was to be a pleasure to serve under his command. So I thought at that time, and I never changed my mind unless it was to increase my admiration for him.

"I had not yet seen this man in action. That treat was to come, and it came very soon. I soon came to the belief that he made no mistakes and whatever he saw fit to encounter was sure to turn out all right. He believed that his troop could not be defeated. His men believed that he could not be defeated. Without this faith in my captain I fear that my rather keen appreciation of the dangers in our encounters with the Indians could not have been concealed. In battle he was always cool, never indulging in high-sounding stuff, to be quoted afterward in newspaper accounts. When action opened we heard his first and last order. It was always the same: 'G Troop, CHARGE.' That was all. The superfluous shouting was all done by the charging men.

"I soon decided that he was my ideal of a commander and that I could wish for none better."

That Private Hardin took advantage of his opportunities in this troop is shown from the fact that from the beginning he rose to the rank of major, which he now holds on the retired list.

There was no affectation about Bernard, as can be readily seen from his record. He made no concealment of the fact that he had risen from the ranks, and the members of his troop were only too well aware that he had started as a blacksmith. It goes without saying that he had the best shod and the best mounted troop in the regiment, for even if he had been given the last choice of horses at every division, he would have come through with the pick of the lot. Of course, horsemanship was his first requirement. Like Fenimore Cooper's hero he saw the

"This man is sick!"

advantage of developing the gifts he had, so was in frequent demand on expeditions to purchase horses, and in 1875 we find him going to San Francisco to receive instruction in the "Goodenough" manner of horseshoeing, which he was ordered to adopt.

"It is all damned nonsense," he told his troop farrier, on his return, "but we'll have to use the shoes somehow."

The "Goodenough" horseshoe was rather thick in front and thin in rear, and the instructions were to magnify this effect by cutting down the heel and frog of the horse's foot as low as possible. "This, if carried out, would have the same effect as the removal of the heel of the boot of a man accustomed to high heels would have on the man," according to the troop farrier of that period. "We decided upon a policy by which we hoped to use the shoes without crippling the horses. We reversed the system, leaving the rear part of the hoof as high as possible, and cutting down the toe as much as was safe. Thus, by having a captain who was also a horseshoer we saved our horses, and we used the shoes until brains returned to the skulls of the proper authorities. In another company of the regiment the captain loyally obeyed orders and all of his horses were crippled."

Besides horsemanship, Bernard paid attention to marksmanship, although little official provision was then made for training in the rifle, carbine or revolver. In an earlier period soldiers were marched to a rifle range after every tour of guard duty, and there they unloaded their muzzle-loaders by firing them at a target. After the advent of breech-loaders, provision was made for occasional firing of a course of three shots at a three-inch bull's-eye, the range being one hundred yards. But a certain amount of ammunition could be expended in hunting, and Bernard was never known to refuse a hunting pass, and always provided plenty of ammunition. He liked to hunt himself, and often took his turn at it on expeditions. By example and precept he encouraged good shooting at every opportunity. Later the army adopted the Creedmoor system of rifle practice, which was much more effective.

Bernard also devoted much time to training his troop with the saber, a weapon he had found effective at Smithfield and in other battles of the Civil War, although not of much use in Indian campaigns. It was not carried in the Modoc, Bannock, Sheepeater and Apache campaigns, but in 1876, when the troop was brought from San Diego to Solidad Pass after the Custer disaster, expectant of orders to move by railroad to the scene of the Sioux campaign. instructions were given to take sabers, and it was planned to try them out against the Sioux. But Bernard's troop was too far away to get a chance at action in this war.

Of powerful physique, Bernard was not an unusually large man, being about five feet, ten inches in height and weighing about one hundred and eighty pounds. At this time he was wearing the full beard so common in the post Civil War period. His hair and beard were black, slightly streaked with gray. He was a soldierly, erect figure, with broad shoulders. An incident of the Bannock War illustrates his physical fitness. It was at the end of a sixty mile night march. It may be remarked that half this distance is a very fair day's ride for cavalry. A number of officers were grouped about him on the ground when camp had been made, and there was considerable grumbling, probably not intended to be fault-finding but just the usual soldier-talk of being a little sorry for oneself because one's exertions and hardships were so little appreciated. Bernard listened to just

Turned a handspring, lighting on his feet.

so much of this without remark, and then all he said was:

"Well, I'm the oldest man here." (He was then 45).

Slowly he arose to his feet, straightened up, and turned a handspring, lighting on his feet "with the grace of a circus acrobat" according to Lieutenant W. C. Brown, who tells the story. Of course the grumbling ceased.

There is another story that illustrates his physical possibilities. A sentry having difficulty with a prisoner at Fort McDermit, Nevada, called for the corporal of the guard. Bernard went out to see what the row was about. The drunken prisoner resented interference, called Bernard by some vile names, and made a lunge at him. An officer is not supposed to strike an enlisted man, and Bernard did not. Instead he caught the prisoner in both hands, lifted him off the ground, and shook him as a terrier shakes a rat, then threw him flat on his back on the ground.

"Sergeant, take this man away and sober him up," he ordered, and hurried away somewhat ashamed of having so far lost his temper. But the prisoner hardly needed any further sobering-up process. He was ready to behave. As a result he was released next day; Bernard preferred no charges.

There is another story told that illustrates how Bernard was at one with his men. While not prescribed in tables of organization, it is an ancient "custom of the service" that each company in the army—and during all this period a troop of cavalry was still officially a "company" —is entitled to one dog. Jack, a setter, had attached himself to Company G some time before the Sheepeater campaign. He attended all mounted drills and regularly posted himself as herd guard. He served with honor throughout the campaign, and was a true troop dog, showing no partiality for any one of his half a hundred masters. Officially, however, Jack did not exist, and Bernard apparently ignored him.

The next year, upon changing station from Boise Barracks to Fort McDermit, Jack was among the missing. There was a dark suspicion that a company of the Twenty-first Infantry remaining at the barracks, had kidnapped Jack. No enlisted man dared suggest returning for the dog, but at the first halt Bernard wanted to know what had become of Jack. When the suspicion was explained he suggested that a sergeant take one man and return for Jack. Private Riley was selected as the most capable, and the two set forth, prepared, if need be, to battle an entire company of infantry to recover Jack.

No such heroism was necessary, however. When the pair approached their old barracks and whistled, Jack came bolting through the orderly room window, bringing the glass with him. Apparently he had been locked up accidentally. He was unhurt, so the three made their way leisurely on the trail of the troop. As they approached the camp, Jack dashed ahead, swam a small stream, and charged down upon his many masters, giving each of them a moist and muddy greeting. About the third or fourth he noticed was the company commander, who was approaching with a wash basin full of water in his hand. Showing a complete disregard for military rank, Jack bounded upon Colonel Bernard, upset the pan of water all over him, and followed that indignity with planting muddy paws all over the officer, much to the horror of the two rescuers. But Bernard showed no displeasure, hugging and petting the dog until Jack dashed away to other friends. This was Jack's *croix de guerre*, and it was much appreciated by the company.

Generally Bernard was fortunate in the lieutenants assigned to his troop. One of the earliest was John Quincy Adams (a native of New York, probably not related to the presidential family) who was first lieutenant during the campaign against Cochise. Adams enlisted as a private in an Ohio regiment at the beginning of the Civil War. He was commissioned in the Signal Corps on March 3, 1863, which is the date of the organization of that branch of service, so he was one of its original officers. And it was he who wig-wagged its most famous message "Hold the fort for I am coming," as the gospel hymn has it, from Sherman to Corse at Allatoona. He was brevetted first lieutenant and captain during the Civil War. Although no longer assigned to Company G, Lieutenant Adams was still in the First Cavalry at the time of the Modoc War and had charge of the signal station that overlooked the scene of the murder of General Canby and gave the alarm after that attack. Adams remained in the regiment until his retirement as captain in 1896.

Lieutenant Winters seemed to be one of Bernard's favorites, an officer of much initiative and capability in field command. John G. Kyle as second lieutenant displayed good qualities in the Modoc War, commanding the troop for a time. Frederick K. Ward succeeded Winters as first lieutenant. In later years he became an inspector general. John Pitcher was notable in the Bannock war and performed valuable services in the Sheepeater campaign. "No man could wish for better officers than these," says an enlisted man who served under nearly all of them. "Of course, there were many other excellent officers in the regiment, but the men of our troop, being satisfied with what we had, wanted no others. This, of course, was just a bit of silly prejudice, but entertaining it was good for the morale of the troop." Also it was not altogether common for all the officers of a troop to be recognized by its personnel as the best they could possibly get. Much of this is due, no doubt, to Bernard's training.

Another officer who figures in these pages is Lieutenant W. C. Brown. He was not an officer of Bernard's troop, but served under Bernard's command in both the Bannock and Sheepeater campaigns. He had a notable career in the army, commanding the Tenth Cavalry during Pershing's Punitive Expedition into Mexico, and serving overseas as inspector, Quartermaster Corps, during the World War. He was promoted to brigadier general on the retired list in 1927. He relates an incident of the Bannock War that reveals something of Bernard's methods.

"I was a young lieutenant and only joined in December, 1877. I had abundance of good health and ignorance, but the conditions were such that I learned rapidly. Immediately upon arrival at Wild Horse Creek July 14, 1878, Colonel Bernard, Lieutenant Winters, and I were detailed as members of a board to estimate the value of a wheat field about two hundred yards away in which it was proposed to turn the horses to graze. We soon decided one hundred dollars was its value and I mounted my horse to ride back to camp, when Bernard spoke sharply:

" 'What are you doing?'

" 'I'm going to ride back to camp and unsaddle.'

" 'You are a fine soldier! You've ridden that horse over sixty miles and when right at the grazing ground you propose to ride him back to camp! Do you see what we are doing?'

"I *then* noticed that Bernard and Winters were unsaddling and preparing to turn their horses loose in the wheat field. I sheepishly dismounted, unsaddled and carried my saddle and pack back to camp."

[91]

VII

CAPTAIN JACK AND THE MODOCS*

"BLACK JACK" RAYMOND, first sergeant of Company G, First Cavalry, fidgeted uncomfortably while from the corner of his eye he watched Colonel Bernard read the brief order that had that moment arrived from Fort Klamath. The scout who brought it was standing, first on one foot, then on the other, across the orderly room, wondering if he dared follow frontier custom in making himself at home in the presence of Bernard, who had a fighting reputation that even a frontiersman would respect. But the suspense was not long enough to cause either of the observers much time for reflection. Bernard's order was given quietly and was obeyed quickly.

"It's an expedition, sergeant. Three—better make it four—days' rations. Usual post guard to stay."

"About twenty men, sir?"

"Eighteen ought to be enough this time. Give two more men a chance against the Modocs."

"Modocs!" That was what Sergeant Raymond wanted to know, as he took his duty roster and went over to the barracks. He recalled vaguely a small tatterdemalion

*BIBLIOGRAPHY: *Northwestern Fights and Fighters,* by C. T. Brady (New York, 1907); *The Story of the Soldier,* by Bvt. Brig. Gen. George A. Forsyth (New York, 1900); Final Report of Bvt. Maj. Gen. A. C. Gillem in U. S. Senate Spec. Session, Mar. 5, 1877, Ex. Doc. 1; "Gosh Dash It, Let's Charge," by Maj. C. B. Hardin in *Winners of the West,* May 30, 1933; Address, "The Modoc War of 1872-73," by Brigadier General James T. Kerr, before the Order of Indian Wars of the United States, Jan. 24, 1931; *Wigwam and War-Path,* by A. B. Meacham (Boston, 1873); *Reminiscences of a Pioneer,* by Col. William Thompson (San Francisco, 1912); *Lava Beds National Monument,* United States Department of Agriculture, Forest Service; *Indian History of the Modoc War,* by Jeff C. Riddle (1914).

band along Lost River. Fortunately there wouldn't be much trouble with them, he thought. It was only a small tribe of rebels from the Klamath Reservation that couldn't get along with its more powerful kinfolk, the Klamaths. Sergeant Raymond was a good garrison soldier who had little liking for serious field service. He had recently succeeded to the diamond upon the retirement of Francis Oliver, a fine old soldier, but was not to wear it long, for Bernard's troop seldom was kept at dress parade duty. Raymond was quick enough in detailing the guard to remain at Fort Bidwell and in sending the rest of the company in a mad scramble to get its field equipment together.

Colonel Bernard knew that General Canby, his commanding officer of New Mexican Civil War campaigns, now department commander, had received complaints about the band that was living along the Lost River Valley. Settlers in that area had made some wild charges, but when pinned down could prove nothing more serious than a few cases of petty thievery. The general had not taken the complaints very seriously. The Indian agents had wanted the Modoc band brought back to the Klamath Reservation, but the Modocs and Klamaths were too close akin to get along well together. The Modocs, being the weaker party, had got the worst of it. There had been an incident of some Modocs cutting some rails and a party of Klamaths coming along with a wagon, loading up the rails, and coolly driving off with them. The Indian agent's solution of this and other problems was to move the Modocs to another part of the Reservation, but after two or three such removals the Modocs were pretty well disgusted with their official home. Captain Jack, a Modoc chief, had killed a Klamath medicine man for the reason, very logical to the Indian mind, that the witch doctor had failed to cure a suffering Modoc. The Klamaths wanted to invoke the recently adopted white man's idea of justice against Captain Jack, but the Modocs had no faith in it, and for these sufficient reasons decided to return to their old haunts along Lost River. They were even less romantic looking than Apaches, wore white men's clothes, and tried to act civilized.

Bernard now learned that Captain James Jackson with thirty-five men of Company B, First Cavalry, four packers and a small pack train, had been ordered to get to the Modoc camp, arrest their leaders, and drive the tribe back to its reservation. Jackson had marched all night and struck the Indian camp on Lost River at about daylight. The Indians were ordered to surrender and lay down their arms. When they hesitated, Lieutenant Frazier A. Boutelle moved forward to enforce the order, and fire was opened almost simultaneously on both sides, according to Lieutenant Boutelle's account. A charge drove the Indians out of the village and perhaps eight or nine were killed. The troop lost one man killed and seven wounded. Meanwhile a party of civilians became involved in a fight with the Modocs at Crawley's ranch. After two of the settlers were killed, they called on the troop for help. The Indians hung on until night, and then went into the Lava Beds. On their way they killed some sixteen settlers, but it is notable that they injured no women or children.

Snow, bad roads, and the necessity of taking two wagons made this journey of Company G in December of 1872 a slow one. But within two days it came in sight of the Lava Beds. At that time Tule Lake, a small body of water, lay across the California-Oregon boundary. In the years that have passed since then the Lost

"It's an expedition, sergeant."

River has been found by some engineers who have carried it off bodily, leaving Tule Lake as dry as the Lava Beds that are south of it. As dry, but not quite as useless. In fact, so useless are the Lava Beds that they have been designated the Lava Beds National Monument as a memorial to an Indian war that eighty-seven per cent of the population of the United States never heard of. There are forty-five thousand acres, or about seventy square miles in this reservation, which should settle the per-plexed question of most of the Modoc War accounts as to the approximate area of "hell with the fire out." By actual count in a survey by the Civilian Conservation Corps in the summer of 1933 there were two hundred and twenty-four caves, sixteen sizable volcanic craters, and seventy-five fumeroles, or small mud craters, in this area. These figures are much less subject to disagreement than the number of casualties in any battle of the Modoc War, each commentator having original ideas on this subject. But there is reason for the many controversies.

The saucy Confederate of 1861 traditionally thought

himself able to lick five Yanks. After four years of Civil War he was willing to reduce his boast to something like two and a half, and he won considerable fame for attempting that much. But when a Modoc—an Indian so insignificant looking that he did not even wear a war bonnet and a lot of beads—not only claimed, but proved he could lick ten soldiers, one might expect a considerable explosion of literary fireworks. The flares soon burned out and the ashes of the controversy have been covered with dust, so that a considerable search must be made for the pale light of truth under the bushel of alibis. This is less necessary on Bernard's side of Jack's cave.

When Bernard reported to Major John Green of the First Cavalry at Crawley's Ranch, he was joined there by ten men of his own troop under Lieutenant J. G. Kyle, who had come from detached duty at Fort Warner with Company F, commanded by Captain David Perry, Bernard's associate of Civil War days. A total force of about four hundred was assembled, B, F, G and H of the First Cavalry; B, C and F of the Twenty-first Infantry; Companies A and B of Oregon Volunteers, twenty-four Volunteer Riflemen from California, and a company of Klamath Indian Scouts. Lieutenant Colonel Frank Wheaton of the Twenty-first Infantry was in command.

Some fear was expressed that there would not be enough Indians to go around. Captain Jack's band is variously estimated at from forty to one hundred and twenty, with about seventy-five or eighty as a fair guess. The soldiers were soon to find that this was quite enough.

Bernard's troop was sent to Land's Ranch at the northeast corner of the Lava Beds, about eight miles from Jack's stronghold, to prevent the Modocs from leaving by that route. The Modocs had no intention of leaving by any route just then, and, if they had, Bernard's troop would have been in a bad spot. But I cannot imagine he was disappointed in these orders. Major Green and Captain Perry, his immediate superiors, were good and sufficient officers, with many affairs to their credit, but neither had the mercuric, explosive temperament that Colonel Bernard liked to work with. When Jackson's troop was sent to him a few days later, Bernard was well pleased. Jackson and his second lieutenant, Frazier A. Boutelle, had not done so well in their Lost River fight that started the war. Bernard liked to have men under him who had a score to even off. James Jackson was a short, stocky figure, somewhat in-clined to corpulency, a bewhiskered, unromantic looking officer, but steady and cool, a very Porthos in action, as he later demonstrated in the Nez Perce war of 1877 when he brought a pack train through the Indians' line at the battle of the Clearwater.

Captain James Jack-son, 1st Cavalry

On December 21st came the first skirmish. The Modocs attacked a supply wagon with an escort of five men from Fort Bidwell. Bernard led a handful of men to the rescue, about a half mile from his camp, and drove off the Indians. Private Sydney A. Smith was killed and Private William Donahue wounded so severely that he died the next day.

Bernard was eager to get into action. The Lava Beds appeared to him no tougher nut to crack than Cochise's stronghold in the Chiricahuas. Jackson's fight had taken place on November 29th; January arrived and nothing had been done. Major Green counseled patience. "So far as moving on the Indians is concerned, I am as anxious as you possibly can be, but the District Commander has decided to await the arrival of the Howitzers before moving (believing that they will save many lives) over which I have no more control than you have," he wrote from the other side of the lava caves. The howitzers had been delayed by the "horrid condition of the road"—complained of by some of the troops that pushed through the mountains to join the expedition. Wagons had been sent out to assist the section of mountain howitzers, and their arrival was promised for January 13th. Lieutenant W. H. Miller of the First Cavalry was given charge of them.

But at last plans were drawn for a battle to begin in the early morning of January 17th. Bernard's two troops, G under Lieutenant Kyle and B under Captain Jackson, were to advance from the east, while the remaining cavalry, infantry and volunteers under Colonel Wheaton were to move from the west, join both their wings with those of Bernard, and surround the Modocs. But in all the time that had elapsed evidently little reconnaissance had been made of the ground to be fought over.

Colonel Bernard, however, took no chances. Hours before daylight on the morning of January 16th he moved out to take position for an attack that was planned for the early morning of January 17th. He did not know the location of the Indians; he knew little of the character of the ground, so he allowed plenty of time for finding a suitable line of departure. It was well that he did so. The night was very dark when Companies B and G left Land's Ranch, and progress toward the stronghold in the Lava Beds was slow. When daylight arrived, it brought a dense fog through which one could see scarcely fifty yards. The distance to be traveled was not more than ten miles, but it was well past noon before this much had been made. Then the barking of dogs warned Bernard that he was not far from Captain Jack's stronghold.

But he was prepared for this. Already his men were deployed as skirmishers (horses had been left in camp, as it was impossible for them to maneuver in the Lava Beds). As the first barking of the dogs was heard, the entire line, spread at five-yard intervals, was ordered to lie down. There was din and commotion from the Modoc camp, and while the troops waited to see what would happen next, the fog lifted and they could see the Indians, mostly women and children, leaping about and shouting defiance. And it so happened that this was the only time the Modocs were seen until long after the two-day battle was over.

Bernard had, in effect, made a reconnaissance in force. He had discovered the Indian position, and he was now ready to draw back until the time set for the general attack. He ordered a retreat as skirmishers by companies —first Troop B would face about, run some fifty yards, halt and face the enemy; then Troop G would do the same thing, the troopers of one company or the other keeping the Modocs under constant fire from a prone position, quite in a manner prescribed in books of tactics today.

As this move started, the Indians opened up a brisk fire from the protection of rocks all along the front. They poured over the rocks and gained a position to the left and rear of Bernard's line, from where they began shooting at the pack train. Bernard ordered a charge, and the

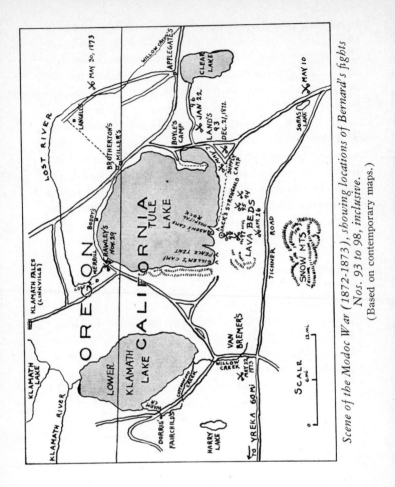

Scene of the Modoc War (1872-1873), showing locations of Bernard's fights Nos. 93 to 98, inclusive.

(Based on contemporary maps.)

troops went in with a rush, driving off the Modocs, who then and there decided that they had a bear by the tail and had better let him go. Three men were wounded up to this time, but Bernard's two companies were unmolested in a further retreat of a half mile to Hospital Rock, so called because the wounded were there cared for, and camp was made for the night and preparations completed for the attack on the morrow.

Leaving a guard of five men with the three wounded and the pack train, Bernard moved out at dawn of January 17th with a hundred officers and enlisted men. Again a dense fog hung over the Lava Beds and nothing could be seen of the Indians. As the point of advance of the day before was reached, the two companies were met by a blast of rifle fire from every angle, but not a Modoc could be seen.

"Charge," Bernard shouted. But as he did so, Lieutenant Kyle, commanding Company G, cried out, "Colonel, I'm hit." Bernard called to Captain Jackson, asking him to send Lieutenant Boutelle to take charge of G. In this first fire, besides the lieutenant, wounded, one enlisted man was killed and four wounded. Seeing that an advance was impossible, Bernard drew his entire line back to better cover some distance in the rear.

And there it stayed. Hugging the cold rocks that became icy after three hours of inaction, the troopers were unable to see any trace of their hidden foe through the damp fog that continued to hang over the Lava Beds until late in the day.

Meanwhile, from the other side, a stronger column went into action. Captain Perry led the advance with the cavalry. Just as his force came under fire, and attempted a charge, it found itself faced by a deep chasm. At the only possible crossing the Modocs had established what we would now call a "strong point," and soon Perry's troopers found themselves trapped. They were compelled to call upon the infantry for help. When the line was straightened out after the rescue of the cavalry it was found to be still a long way from connecting with Bernard. Major Green now tried to establish this connection through moving by the left flank.

Meanwhile Bernard had attempted to assist Green's attack, or at least create a diversion, by a movement to his left. He formed his two companies at five-yard intervals under shelter of the shelf of rock behind which they had been lying. Then he marched them cautiously to the left. An advance of about three hundred yards was made, which was abandoned, probably because the head of the column ran upon a section of the impossible gorge manned so effectively by the Modocs. Bernard's troops were marched back to their original positions. A heavy fire had been poured upon them during all of this movement, but fortunately most of the Indians shot too high.

Shortly after this movement, or about an hour before sundown, the fog lifted, and Bernard was able to see and talk to Green's forces, now attempting to break through between the lake and Jack's Cave. The howitzers had been fired intermittently during the day, but most of their shells had gone entirely over the Modoc position, some of them falling dangerously near Bernard's lines. Word was passed back for them to cease fire. They were manned, of course, by cavalry and infantry untrained in use of these weapons.

Major Green now made a determined effort to break through to Bernard. The Modocs concentrated their fire on his line, so effectively that they succeeded in breaking it after a large section of it had broken through along the lake front. From this time on the soldiers were content to hold the positions they had until dark, when all were withdrawn, Green marching his command back with that of Bernard, and the next day taking a long roundabout course to his original camp at Van Brimmer's ranch.

During the entire day the soldiers had not seen an Indian. Although they had kept up a heavy fire, it is doubtful if a single Modoc had been hit. On the other hand the troops suffered very severely, the heaviest loss falling on the battalion of the Twenty-first Infantry. The total is given as sixteen enlisted men killed and nine officers and forty-four enlisted men wounded.

Bernard had done all that was expected of him. He had not been defeated at any point and his loss had been small. He had withdrawn only when ordered to do so. In his report to Major Green he had no hesitancy in offering suggestions for the further conduct of the campaign. "I have wished respectfully to say that the place the Indians now occupy cannot be taken by a less force than 700 men and to take the place by an assault with this force will cost half the force in killed and wounded," he estimated, and Colonel Wheaton adopted his figure. "A large force, well supplied, judiciously handled, moving at night by approaches, piling up rocks to protect themselves during the day, may take the place." Even from an arm chair, one can hardly criticize this plan of campaign. One feels that Bernard would have been quite at home in the World War. His plan was about what was adopted, but after many delays. "Howitzers could be very effectively used on the east side of the Lava Beds," he says. The long-awaited howitzers had done very little from the west side in the battle of January 17th, except to cause trouble for Bernard, and perhaps this is his gentle hint that he could use them if no one else wanted to.

One is also inclined to wonder if that phrase "judiciously handled" set very well with Bernard's superiors. I suspect sometimes that he was not popular with some of his commanders and colleagues. He was too uniformly right. For the same reason his lieutenants and his troopers swore by him.

He gives a long list of commendations for bravery in action. Since Captain Jackson and Lieutenant Boutelle had won little credit for their affair that started all this trouble, it might be mentioned that the captain was especially commended for going into the field when he should have gone to the hospital. He was so sick that several times he fell to the ground from exhaustion, but remained with his troop during the entire action. There is no reason for doubting Jackson's courage. Boutelle is praised for coolness under the severest fire from the Modoc Caves and for efficiency in commanding Troop G after Kyle was wounded. Kyle was equally praised. Of course, such commendations are customary, and too much weight should not be attached to them.

The results of this unsuccessful attack were various, but not surprising. Colonel A. C. Gillem of the First Cavalry was given command and General Canby came to the scene in person. This was army reaction to defeat after long preparation. But the long list of casualties gave authorities at Washington something else to think about. They questioned whether the result to be obtained was worth its probable cost. If some thought had been given to this phase of the matter before Jackson was airily ordered out to round up this band, there might have been no war. The present result of profound cogitations on the other side of the continent was instructions to hold the troops strictly on the defensive while some effort was made to find out what the Modocs wanted, aside from being let alone. General Canby pointed out that it was a little late in the day to be thinking of this. He knew that the Indians would be feeling their oats after their successful defense of the caves, and that it was a poor time for peace talk. But a commission was appointed and the troops were withdrawn from the Lava Beds while awaiting its arrival.

Bernard moved from Land's Ranch about nine miles to Applegate's Ranch on Clear Lake, January 20th. Two days later the Modocs made a raid on two wagons carrying grain from Tule Lake to Applegate's Ranch and drove off their escort, but Bernard brought troops to the rescue, killed one Indian, wounded several, and sent the rest scurrying back to their caves. Through February and March Bernard's troop remained at Applegate's Ranch. Other troops were arriving at the Lava Beds. Company K of the First Cavalry and Company I of the Twenty-first Infantry joined the detachments of their regiments already in the field. Batteries A, E, K and M of the Fourth Artillery brought up a section of coehorn mortars, another section manning the howitzers, and the rest serving as infantry. Companies E and G of the Twelfth Infantry also joined Gillem's force.

Meanwhile the peace negotiations were dragging slowly along. As General Canby had predicted, the Modocs were by no means willing to talk terms, but, despite his pessimism, Canby seemed so much the most effective of the negotiators that the Department of the Interior, traditionally suspicious of generals, gave him full authority to reorganize the commission if he so desired. However, he had no changes to make. There was some suspicion that the Modocs contemplated treachery and the troops were moved back into the Lava Beds. But

Canby did not believe the Indians would go so far as to murder the commissioners. He thought the Modocs would realize what would be the result of such action. But they had little conception of the power of the United States. They thought that if they killed the chiefs now in the field, the tribes warring against them would disintegrate.

A Peace Tent was erected on the west side of the Lava Beds. It was within view of a signal station near Gillem's tent. There Captain Jack and his leaders were to meet the commission of April 11th, both parties to be unarmed.

In Major E. C. Mason's camp G Troop was on guard. Private Charles B. Hardin was sentry of the first relief on the post nearest the Modoc stronghold. Lieutenant William L. Sherwood of the Twenty-first Infantry was making the rounds as officer of the day. He was very cheerful.

"This is the last day of the war and now we can all go home," he said to the sentry.

But Private Hardin took a more gloomy view of the peace parley. He had heard camp rumors that Toby Riddle, who with her husband, a squaw man, was interpreter for the commission, had warned of a Modoc plot to kill all the negotiators.

"This may be the last day of the war, but I don't believe it," he replied. "I think we will have one more good battle before the war ends."

"Oh, nonsense! You must not be

Major Charles B. Hardin. Formerly private of Troop G, 1st Cavalry.

such a croaker. We shall have peace today. He then gave special orders for the post that the sentry should be friendly to any Modocs who might appear and try to call them into camp. If they would not come in, the sentry was to call the sergeant of the guard, who would notify the officer of the day.

In a short time two Indians appeared, waving a white flag. Private Hardin tried to carry out his instructions, but the Modocs made no haste to come into camp. The lieutenant saw what was going on and came to the sentry post.

"I am going out to see what they want," he said.

The sentry begged Sherwood not to go, but seeing that the officer was determined, began making a loophole in the stone wall that was in front of him, sat down behind it, and covered one of the Modocs with a .50 caliber Sharp's carbine while the talk was going on. Soon the lieutenant returned and notified the sentry that the Indians would return at about 1 o'clock, as they wished to talk with Major Mason, Colonel Bernard and Captain Jackson.

"I thought so," said Hardin.

"What do you mean?"

"I mean they let you go so they might catch bigger game."

Evidently Colonel Bernard did not feel himself delegated to carry on separate peace negotiations, and the other officers called for felt the same way about it. None of them appeared at the time designated, so Lieutenant Sherwood, with Lieutenant W. H. Boyle of his regiment, went out to meet the Indians. Both parties were unarmed. Their conference was short. The Modocs turned back toward the caves to the point where they had left their rifles, seized them, and opened fire on the officers, who meanwhile had started running toward the camp. At the sound of shots the guard was formed, but an excited officer who knew nothing of the case started taking the guard in the wrong direction. Hardin, at the orders of his sergeant, dropped out and went to the point where he had last seen Sherwood, finding him on the ground, wounded. He called the guard, and the lieutenant was carried back to camp. The other officer meanwhile had escaped from the Indians.

At the same time the signal flag was seen to be wildly waving from the signal station, shots were heard from the direction of the Peace Tent, and soon the troops learned that General Canby and the Rev. Dr. Eleazer Thomas, a Methodist clergyman of Petaluma, California, and former missionary, were killed. A. B. Meacham, former superintendent of Indian affairs for Oregon and chairman of the commission was shot four times, but his life and scalp were saved by the Modoc woman Toby Riddle who shouted that the troops were coming. Meacham lived to write a book about the Modoc War and a fourth member of the commission, L. S. Dyer, Indian agent at the Klamath Reservation, who had thoughtfully carried a derringer to the meeting, lived to fight another day in the method traditionally prescribed. Riddle escaped, and Toby was allowed to go. The troops arrived at the scene and rescued Meacham, but too late to catch any Modocs. Mason's command was also going into action, and the war might have ended that day—with a long casualty list— had not Colonel Gillem and Major Mason halted the action. Lieutenant Sherwood died three days later.

Colonel Gillem wasted no time in preparing for a new assault on Captain Jack's stronghold, somewhat along the same lines as the attack of January 17th. At dawn April

15th Major Mason's infantry battalion and Colonel Bernard's two troops were to attack from the east, and in line with Bernard's suggestion the howitzers were assigned to this wing. On the west Major Green was in charge of three troops of the First Cavalry, the artillery serving as infantry, the companies of the Twelfth Infantry and the section of 12-pound coehorn mortars. All that day there continued the same sort of action as in the earlier fight, with the two lines unable to form a junction. But the troops held their positions that night, and all night long the mortars dropped shells into Jack's stronghold. Next morning the attack was resumed, and during this day the two lines were brought together, cutting off the Modocs from their water supply, Tule Lake. That night the Indians tried desperately to pierce the line, but failed. On the morning of April 17th the advance was cautiously resumed, and it was soon found that the Modocs had left the caves, only a small rear guard of snipers remaining. These were quickly driven off. Bernard brought his troop into the stronghold with a loss of only one man wounded.

Cavalry and Indian scouts were unable to find any trace of the Modocs in the immediate vicinity of the stronghold. It was not until April 26th that a command was sent out toward a reported position of the hostiles. This reconnaissance resulted in the final disaster of the campaign, one of which the army is by no means proud. Meanwhile Colonel Bernard became ill and was forced to return to Fort Bidwell, leaving command of his troop to Lieutenant Kyle, who had recovered from his wound, until the first lieutenant, Winters, could arrive from the post.

On April 26th Captain Evan Thomas with two batteries of the Fourth Artillery acting as infantry and a company of the Twelfth Infantry was sent to reconnoiter the supposed position of Captain Jack's camp, with a view to locating positions for the howitzer battery. None of these organizations was much experienced in Indian warfare, and their flank guards showed a disposition to keep too close to the main body. While the party was halted for lunch it was attacked by the Modocs and a large portion of the command was stampeded. Those who remained to fight were killed. Captain Thomas and Lieutenants Albion Howe and Arthur Cranston of the Fourth Artillery, Lieutenant Thomas F. Wright of the Twelfth Infantry, and eighteen enlisted men were among the dead. Bernard's troop, under Kyle, was with the rescuing party that reached the field early next morning, in time to save nineteen wounded. These were brought back with great difficulty. Among them was Lieutenant George M. Harris of the artillery who was so severely injured that he lived only until May 12th.

Brevet Major General Jefferson C. Davis, somewhat notable in the Civil War, succeeded Canby in command and pushed a vigorous campaign. Captain H. C. Hasbrouck, with his Light Battery B of the Fourth Artillery, acting as cavalry, and Jackson's and Bernard's troops of the First Cavalry, went to Dry Lake or Soras Lake at the south end of the Lava Beds, where they were surprised by the Modocs early in the morning of May 10th. "Bernard was not there, but his pupil was," says Private Hardin, for Quartermaster Sergeant Thomas Kelly, without waiting for orders, shouted, "Gosh dash it, let's charge" (his actual words, by unimpeachable authority, little as you may believe it), and Captain Hasbrouck had to speed to get in the lead of his command. Of his force of fifty, five were killed and twelve wounded, but for the first time the Modocs were badly beaten, although driven back again into the Lava Beds.

From this time on it was a fight of small detachments attempting to run down the enemy wherever found. The troops pressed upon the hostiles so closely and so constantly that at last the Modocs deserted their stronghold and scattered. Hasbrouck's force struck the largest party on May 18th near Butte Creek, and a last time May 30th in Langell's Valley, across the Oregon line. As a result of these operations, and those of other columns under Jackson and Perry, most of the Modocs surrendered. Captain Jack was seized a few days later.

After trial by a military commission Captain Jack and three of his followers were hanged for the murders of General Canby and Dr. Thomas. Two others were sentenced to life imprisonment. The remaining prisoners were sent to a reservation in Indian Territory.

After the Modoc War there were several years of comparative inaction for Bernard's troop. During this period Bernard performed a variety of duties—traveled one hundred and ninety-four miles to Adin, California, after stolen horses, went to Camp Warner to confer with the Indian chief Ochoho about going on the Klamath Reservation, went to Fort McDermit in command of an escort to Paymaster Major C. J. Sprague, and commanded an expedition that mapped the country between Fort Bidwell and Fort McDermit. In 1875 the company was moved to the Presidio of San Francisco and subsequently to San Diego Barracks. A fifth child, Mary Alice, was born to the Bernards at Fort Bidwell and a sixth, George Reuben, at San Diego. George died in 1896 at Knoxville, Tennessee. Mary Alice Bernard is now the wife of Colonel Walter C. Babcock.

The move from San Francisco to San Diego was made

on Christmas Day—most of Bernard's Yuletide celebrations appear to have been held in the saddle—on receipt of news of a raid on El Campo, a border town, by some Mexicans. This alarm proved to be of little consequence, but a guard was maintained at El Campo in the expectation of further trouble. It was not until July 22d that the telegraph brought news of another raid on El Campo by Mexicans and Indians. The troop had just removed the shoes from all its horses to give their hoofs a rest, and every horseshoer in San Diego, including the troop farriers, was pressed into service to re-shoe the command. They worked for twenty-four hours without stop and the next morning at seven o'clock the task was completed. At that hour the troop started on its fifty-mile march, arriving at El Campo at three that afternoon.

There Bernard found all the citizens of the surrounding country assembled with their families, wildly excited about the reported raid. He persuaded them that there was no great danger, and marched across the line to the assembly of Mexicans and Indians to discover what the trouble was. He found that the Mexicans and Indians were as much afraid of the Americans as the settlers were of the invading party, so succeeded in quieting all parties for the time being, and returned to El Campo.

The next morning he awoke to find the situation reversed. During the night an Indian had killed a Mexican, and by morning the entire Indian aggregation, men, women, and children, horses, mules, and baggage, was in El Campo seeking the protection of the troops. Again Bernard proved diplomat, and eventually succeeded in sending all three parties home.

It was just after this affair that the troop was moved to the railhead in expectation of taking part in the Sioux campaign. This failed to develop and the troop remained in Southern California until 1877. That year Chief Joseph led the Nez Perces on a long chase from Idaho through Yellowstone Park and Wyoming to the northern boundary of Montana with a considerable portion of the United States Army moving after him from all directions. It was a long way from San Diego to Idaho, but Bernard's troop was ordered out June 27th, marched to Anaheim, took the railroad to Winnemucca, Nevada, marched again to Fort McDermit, and from there to Boise Barracks, Idaho, where it came again under the command of Major John Green. Green's battalion moved to Croesdale's Ranch, near Mount Idaho, but had no luck in catching up with the elusive Nez Perces. After a period of outpost duty at Elk City under Captain E. V. Sumner, the troop went to White Bird Canyon to bury the dead of Captain Perry's troop, which had been severely handled by the Nez Perces there. By this time Chief Joseph and his band had been rounded up far to the north, and Bernard's troop was ordered to take station at Boise Barracks.

VIII

THE BANNOCK WAR*

"THIS is the strangest outbreak I have ever known," wrote Colonel Bernard in one of his early reports on the Bannock War. "They give no reason of any kind for their actions (excepting the Bannocks, who have made some objections to white men coming on Big Camas Prairie with stock). It seems that the several bands conferred together and decided upon an outbreak solely for plunder."

It was not quite as bad as that. There were times when Indians went to war without adequate excuse. But so far as some bands at least were concerned, there was good reason for the Bannock uprising.

Early in the campaign Bernard had heard of the Big Camas Prairie trouble. The camas root formed an important part of the Bannock food supply, and the tribe had no intention of alienating the area where it grew profusely. It is said that the treaty setting aside the Fort Hall reservation included the Camas Prairie as a part of the Bannock lands, but a careless clerk copied it "Kansas" Prairie, and as no one subsequently was able to identify "Kansas Prairie" the reservation line was drawn to exclude Big Camas Prairie. But when the Bannocks found the white man's flocks and herds there, they did not remonstrate, according to the story told Bernard at the start of the trouble. On the contrary, the Indians visited

---

*BIBLIOGRAPHY: *Indian Wars in Idaho,* R. R. Arnold (Caldwell, Ida., 1932); *Life Among the Piutes,* by Sarah Winnemucca Hopkins (Boston and New York, 1883); *My Life and Experiences Among Our Hostile Indians,* by Maj. Gen. O. O. Howard (Hartford, Conn., 1907); *Reminiscences of George Martin Kober,* M.D., LL.D. (Washington, 1930); Statesman *Extra,* Boise City, I. T., June 27, 1878.

the invaders, appeared friendly, and seemingly were in great good humor. Then "without cause or provocation," in the words of Bernard, who held no particular brief for the settler, the Bannocks began shooting.

Sarah Winnemucca of the Piutes tells another story of the trouble at the Fort Hall reservation. She had it only by hearsay, so its value as evidence is doubtful. According to this version of the cause of the outbreak two white men raped an Indian girl; the girl's brother and a companion killed the two white men; authorities at the reservation demanded the surrender of the two Indians to stand charge of murder; the tribe agreed to this and was on the way to give up the two men when they learned that a number of Indians had been imprisoned, probably as hostages. The Bannocks decided that they stood little chance of getting justice—in this they may have been right—and took to the warpath.

Whatever the truth of this story, the Piutes had sufficient occasion for going to war, although no immediate provocation. For several years they had been shifted from one reservation to another, during most of which time they had been exploited and robbed by a succession of incompetent and corrupt agents, and in 1878 were in a condition of near starvation on the Malheur Reservation in Oregon, a long way from their ancestral home in Nevada. Even so Winnemucca, Sarah's father, chief of one of the Piute bands, remained friendly to the whites. Egen, leader of the other band at Malheur, was not enthusiastic for war, but Oytes, "the Dreamer," a medicine man and chief of the Snake River Piutes, was always a trouble maker and managed to enlist many of the Piutes in the uprising.

The Bannocks at Lemhi Reservation of course backed their brothers of Fort Hall and a few Klamaths seem to have gone along for the ride. Most reprehensible were the Umatillas of Oregon, who tried to play both sides and finally treacherously betrayed the hostiles. They were the only party on either side that got anything out of the war, and deserved the least. A few other tribes of Idaho and Oregon were involved.

The originator of this confederation was Buffalo Horn, chief of the Bannocks. He had been a scout leader under General Howard in the Nez Perce war the preceding year, and was inspired by Chief Joseph's successes to attempt to surpass them. Also he was disgusted because the soldiery had failed to annihilate his hereditary enemies, the Nez Perces. It is entirely possible that Buffalo Horn would have built up a great Indian conspiracy, with a bloody war as the consequence, had not the troops acted promptly and successfully. For some strange reason the times when the army succeeded rapidly pass from memory and attain small place in history, while the defeat of Custer and the many other so-called "massacres," the victories of the Nez Perces, and the elusiveness of Geronimo remain subjects for the spilling of tons of ink and alibis.

This is a story of victory without slaughter—a war that Bernard was allowed to fight in his own way.

A messenger arrived at Boise Barracks on May 30, 1878, with news that two herders had been shot by Bannocks at Big Camas Prairie, eighty miles away. At the time that Captain Patrick Collins of the Twenty-first Infantry, commanding the post, was notifying General Howard, the department commander, of the affair, "Boots and Saddles" was sounding at the cavalry barracks. While General Howard was sending telegrams in all directions to start troops on a round-up of the hostiles, and was trying to borrow a few organizations from General Crook's adjoining department, it was reported to him that Colonel Bernard was on his way with Troop G of the First Cavalry, a company of volunteer scouts commanded by Orlando Robbins, a colonel of militia and border character popularly known as "Rube" Robbins, and a few friendly Indians. From this time forward it was General Howard's principal problem to reinforce Bernard.

For Bernard with his fifty troopers was riding boldly into the midst of the Bannock confederation. Boldly, but not carelessly. On the morning of June 1st he reached the Big Camas Prairie and found the two wounded herders. The Bannocks were gone with thirty horses and everything else they could find to steal, and were reported in lava beds seven miles distant, a location much like the scene of the Modoc War. Into this wild region the troop advanced the next day, finding the Indian camp abandoned. So quickly was the trail followed that "other camps were found which had been abandoned in great haste, many important articles being left behind." But the lava beds soon became too rough and too full of rocks for cavalry, so Bernard turned out of them onto the stage road at King Hill Station, which he found deserted and looted, the Indians having stolen ten horses there and cut some pieces of harness into little bits. He pushed on to Glenn's Ferry on the Snake River where he found that the Bannocks had pillaged the house and store, crossed the ferry, and turned the ferry boats loose. On the other side they had looted some freight wagons loaded with hardware, killed one man whose body was found in the river, and stolen several head of horses.

Bernard's conduct of the campaign, as it now developed, was almost the ideal in Indian warfare. Constantly he kept pushing the hostiles, never allowing them to get the impression that anyone was afraid of them, at the same time allowing them no chance at him, and continuously giving them the idea that he was backed by overwhelming force. He was always in touch with General Howard, who had come immediately to Boise Barracks, and kept that officer apprised of every move. This any superior will appreciate, for many officers are so anxious for separate command as to try to keep their movements in the dark, and many others neglect to tell of their position because they have nothing of an unusual nature to report.

But Bernard promptly informed Howard of his discoveries, and of his opinions—that the robbing and horse stealing were said to have been done by Umatillas and Piutes, and that bands from the Fort Hall and Lemhi Agencies were still in the Lava Beds. "As they go west they will probably commit more depredations and incite other Indians to join them," Bernard reported. "This party, as well as those remaining in the Lava Beds, should be closely watched until a force sufficient to handle them can be assembled. The Indians when all together are reported to number from three hundred to five hundred warriors."

Without further orders Bernard set for himself the task of watching the main band.

Bernard's reports strengthened General Howard's hand exceedingly, for already the over-eager friends of the Indians in the far east were urging the general to negotiate. Howard knew very well that little could be done after the fighting had started. The fate of General Canby should have been sufficient warning of the futility of trying to talk peace with victorious Indians. But when an "officer of experience and ability," as General Howard called Bernard, reported the original outbreak as "without cause or provocation" and stated that the Indians "give no reason of any kind for their actions," but "decided upon an outbreak solely for plunder," there seemed little left to argue. Nevertheless, he was willing to try it if Bernard could find the means.

Meanwhile Captain Collins had been busy at Boise Barracks trying to give Bernard every possible assistance. Collins mounted his own company of the Twenty-first Infantry on animals he was able to scrape together and marched them to Bernard at Snake River, but he himself returned to Boise, probably under orders. It is noticeable that General Howard sent out no company commander who ranked Bernard. With this reinforcement Bernard crossed Snake River, sending Robbins' scouts along the trail while he delayed to escort a party of citizens out of danger to Mundy's Ferry, over Snake River southeast of Boise. On June 8th in a report to the general, Bernard fixed the Indians at Battle Creek, seven miles from South Mountain, and advised the assembly of troops at Silver City.

The Indians were in fact at Battle Creek that day, and there were fought by a party of twenty-six volunteers under Captain J. B. Harper. Accounts of this fight vary considerably in detail, but certainly it is beyond debate that with so small a force discretion might well be considered the better part of the volunteers' valor. From their own accounts you might not suspect it, although they do admit a Fabian withdrawal. But one important result was attained. Buffalo Horn, the leader of the entire uprising, was killed in this trifling skirmish. One "Piute Joe" afterward described the retreat of the volunteers as

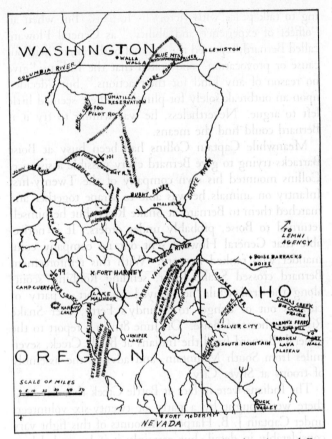

Scene of the Bannock War, 1878; showing locations of Bernard's fights Nos. 99, 100, and 101.

(Based on contemporary maps.)

very precipitate and gives himself credit for saving the day by shooting down Buffalo Horn. All twenty-six of Captain Harper's volunteers agreed that this story sounded highly improbable and noted that the veracity even of friendly Indians was questionable. Be that as it may, the Bannock leader was dead, and his followers were not excelled by the volunteers in leaving the scene of action. The hostiles fled in the direction of the camp of Malheur Piutes in Stein's Mountains, sometimes called Juniper Mountains, as the range is near Juniper Lake.

Bernard continued on the trail to Silver City. There he received Howard's request that an attempt be made to communicate with the hostile band. To this he replied "Concerning the division commander's wish to communicate by scouts with the hostile Bannocks, so far I can get no Indian or other person to attempt such a thing. The Piutes hereabouts and in Duck Valley are all assembled near the whites for protection."

The next day, while marching along the Winnemucca stage road, at a point called the Stone House, Bernard was informed by a volunteer captain that an important capture had been made, no less than a wagon full of ammunition for the hostiles. Perhaps you have never heard that Indians on the warpath had ammunition trains. Neither had Bernard. Yet there was a wagon, and Bernard immediately recognized its driver. She was Sarah Winnemucca, a Piute "princess," daughter of old Chief Winnemucca, one of the most notable Indian characters of her time. For many years she had been interpreter at various reservations to which her tribe was shifted. She was well educated in English and was widely known for her friendship for the whites. In later years she wrote a book of her reminiscences, one of the first books to be written by an Indian, and she lectured widely on the

[121]

wrongs of her people. At this time she was on her way to Washington to complain of the treatment her tribe was receiving at the Malheur Reservation, which she had left a few days before the outbreak.

But her rôle in the Bannock War was not to be that of diplomat. Instead she was to become scout and guide, performing services recognized by the Piutes as entitling her to consideration almost as of the status of chief.

Bernard rode up to her. His manner was a bit gruff.

"Sarah, these citizens say you have a good deal of ammunition in your wagon."

"Captain, they must know or they would not say so. Go and see for yourself, captain, and if you find anything in my wagon besides a knife and fork and a pair of scissors, I will give you my head for a football. How can I be taking guns and ammunition to my people when I am going right away from them? Go to my wagon and see."

"No, Sarah, I believe what you tell me is true."

Sarah beamed.

"Now, captain, you do me a great favor by believing me. If I can be of any use to the army I am at your service, and I will go with it till the war is over."

"Well, Sarah, I will telegraph to General Howard. He is at Fort Boise and I will see what he says about it. Do you know the country pretty well?"

"Yes, of course."

"Well, Sarah, I will send for you from the Sheep Ranch. You will come if I send, will you?"

"I will come if the citizens don't kill me."

"Well, Sarah, I would like to have you go as my guide, for I can get no Indian to go with me for love or money."

"Yes, captain, I will go and do all I can for the government if General Howard wants me."

So from Silver City Bernard telegraphed to the general, "Sarah Winnemucca is in my camp, offering her services for the good of her people. She wants to go to them with any message you or General McDowell might desire to send them. She thinks if she can get to the Piutes with a message from you or General McDowell she could get all the well-disposed of people to come near the troops, where they would be safe and be fed; says there is nothing at the Malheur Agency to feed them with."

And General Howard promptly replied,

"Send Sarah with two or three friendly Indians, if you can get them, to go straight to her people and have them send a few of their principal men to you. I will see myself that all who have behaved and come in are properly fed. Promise Sarah a reward if she succeeds."

Sarah had come into camp with four Indians bearing messages from Fort McDermit, who had refused to accompany her on her proposed expedition to the hostile camp. But the courage of the Piute girl shamed them, and two of them finally agreed to accompany her. Oytes had out-talked and more or less kidnapped Chief Winnemucca and his band into the uprising of Buffalo Horn, and now that Buffalo Horn was dead, Oytes and Egan became leaders of the entire movement. They had decreed death for anyone even bearing a message from the whites, so Sarah faced considerable danger when she entered the hostile camp disguised in war paint and blanket. She managed to reach her father without detection, however, and after she delivered General Howard's message, he agreed to lead his band out of the enemy camp. That night seventy-five Piutes stole away. But soon the followers of Oytes and Egan were on the trail.

Sarah came bursting into Bernard' scamp riding as fast as her horse would carry her—she had come seventy-five miles that day according to her account—shouting for help. She reported that her father was surrounded by the Bannocks. Robbins' scouts rode out and rescued Chief Winnemucca and some of his followers.

Bernard now pushed on toward Stein's Mountains. At the crossing of the Owyhee River he was joined by Company F of his regiment under Lieutenant Peter S. Bomus and Company L under Captain Stephen G. Whipple. Then, with General Howard's approval, he deviated through Barren Valley to join Captain Thomas Mc-Gregor with Company A at Fort Harney. Howard, meanwhile was assembling all the infantry companies he could, and was pushing with them to the front. He was "gratified at the energy displayed by you and your command," he wrote Bernard in an order of June 23d, "and he hopes that you will continue by the same exertion to push the enemy back in the direction of Stein's Mountain and upon our force," but he added in a postscript, "The General desires to be fully advised of these matters as seen from your standpoint," showing that Howard was quite willing to let Bernard manage affairs in his own fashion, if results could be obtained.

But before this order was issued, the situation had changed. At midnight on June 21st Bernard's troops left Fort Harney to attack the Bannock camp on Silver Creek, sixty miles away. They rode most of the next day, halting for the night at a burned ranch. At five o'clock the morning of June 23d the battalion moved out, and within three miles of Robbins' scouts reported sighting the camp, on Silver Creek about thirty-six miles from where it empties into Harney Lake, occupied by about seven hundred Bannocks and Piutes.

Bernard drew up his force in four lines, three of which were to charge in successive waves through the Indian

[124]

camp. This method had an advantage peculiar to Indian warfare. If a man were wounded or dismounted—his horse perhaps shot from under him—another line was in his rear to pick him up. It was a primary principle in Indian warfare never to abandon a wounded man for an instant, for the probability was that he would be killed if left alone. Ordinarily an effort was made to leave no dead bodies to the mutilating habits of the Indians. This made advisable a different system of tactics from that employed in civilized warfare. Other commanders, however, might have attempted to surround the village, charging in from several directions. It is not difficult to recall examples, with unfortunate consequences. But that was not Bernard's way.

The post of honor was given to Company F, Lieutenant Bomus commanding, for that troop had the stain of White Bird Canyon in the Nez Perce War to wipe out. "It has been said that Col. Perry's company would not stand fire," says a contemporary newspaper account. "It was in the lead yesterday and they did well." Bernard's company, G, under Lieutenant Frederick K. Ward, was next and Captain McGregor's Company A was the third line. Company L was in reserve, as a guard to the pack train. When all was ready, Bernard issued the following order:

"I will say to you men that the enemy is close to us; we came here to whip them and we are going to do it. I want you all to keep good order, and no running. If anyone runs I will have him shot, so he might as well die by the enemy as by friends.

"Forward, Not too fast!"

The battalion advanced at a swift canter until within about five hundred yards of the enemy, when the charge was sounded. Companies F and G went in with a rush, and Company A, the troop from Fort Harney that had not taken part in the long chase, having fresh horses, soon caught up with the leaders. The Indians were up and ready, but could not stand the shock of cavalry charge with six-shooter and carbine. Twice Bernard's force galloped through the village, and the hostiles fled for the bluff across the creek. Sergeant George H. Raymond of Company A had a hand-to-hand encounter with Bearskin, a Bannock chief, in the village, the Indian finally being killed with a pistol shot. Bernard had no intention of allowing a disorganized charge on the steep bluffs—some accounts indicate that they were fortified by the Indians, although this seems improbable—so now had the recall sounded, brought the troops back to the pack train to replenish the ammunition supply, and reformed the battalion. Unwilling to take the risk of charging across the creek thickly lined with small willow trees, he now deployed his men as skirmishers and opened a heavy fire on the Indian position. This was continued the rest of the day, and by night the hostiles were much discouraged. They had lost their camp with all its equipment and loot, ammunition and supplies, and there seemed to be little chance of re-taking it. Between midnight and two o'clock they stole away. Bernard reported ten Indians definitely known to be killed and about forty more believed slain. His own loss was four killed and three wounded.

This was the first fight of the campaign—except the indefinite affair at Battle Creek—and it was a notable victory. When the news reached Boise City—four days later—the *Statesman* of that place issued an "extra," an edition only two columns wide containing nothing but "Particulars of Col. Bernard's Battle With the Indians," an unusual recognition during the Indian wars. General

Howard did not have to wait that long for his report of the fight. He was moving vigorously to support Bernard, moving infantry to the front in wagons—anticipating to some degree the much advertised taxicab reinforcement at the Battle of the Marne. Perhaps he was disappointed that Bernard had not been able to drive the Indians toward the infantry, but no hint of it appears in the commendatory order issued—at two o'clock in the morning!—June 25th from Sage Hen Spring. "I am delighted at your success and congratulate your officers and men with all my heart," it said. "The loss of their ammunition and baggage and stores bothers them." Then he tells of the troops being rushed forward and concludes, "I am with Miles and if you do not run them another ten miles, we will be up before night."

But General Howard was destined to be disappointed in this. During the preceding day, June 24th, Bernard had halted only long enough to bury the dead, and then had driven the Indians another ten miles. Shots were exchanged at seven o'clock that evening, but the Bannocks kept moving. Captain Evan Miles' company of the Twenty-first Infantry to which Howard referred, was pushed forward, and Captain Charles Bendire's Company K of the First Cavalry, a day behind at that time, was able to join Bernard in two days' forced marches on June 27th. The five troops now moved through the Blue Mountains and the John Day River valley, keeping the hostiles moving north rapidly. Near the North Fork of the John Day River, General Howard finally caught up July 6th and the pursuit was continued across the fork, through the Blue Mountains, by another Camas Prairie, to Pilot Rock on Birch Creek. Here Company E under Captain W. H. Winters, Bernard's former lieutenant, and Company H under Lieutenant W. R. Parnell joined Bernard, bringing

Continued the advance, firing their carbines, ready to mount and charge again.

his force to seven troops of the First Cavalry. The enemy was now reported close at hand.

At eight o'clock on the morning of July 8th, Bernard's seven companies struck the Indians at a strong position in a mountain about seven miles from Pilot Rock. Howard was present, but gave no orders. It was Bernard's war, and the general was eager to have Bernard fight it to a finish. So eagerly General Howard watched the troops take the trot and begin the ascent of the mountain. Soon the Indians opened fire. A few soldiers and horses were seen to be hit. But "soon we saw them clearing the summit. It was speedily done; wave after wave striking the Indians' position—front and flank—in quick succession," says Howard. But the Indians abandoned this crest, leaving a few worn-out horses and mules, and retreated to a still stronger position. "Bernard was vexed; yes, disgusted," the general noted as the colonel tried vainly to cut off the Indians' retreat. But another charge drove them from this ridge into the timber. Here Bernard gave "the

first example of the fighting cavalry on foot without separating the men from the horses," according to the regimental history. The men dismounted, threw the reins over the forearm, and continued to advance, firing their carbines, ready to mount and charge again if opportunity offered. Officers got into the fight. Lieutenant W. C. Brown, who was present with Company L, says, "I recall taking a carbine from a trooper and trying (unsuccessfully) to pick off some of those Indians who were

2d Lieutenant W. C. Brown, 1st Cavalry. (Taken about 1880.)

[129]

audaciously 'circling' on their ponies and trying to draw our fire at about eight hundred yards," quite a long range for a carbine.

The Indians were steadily pushed back until about 12:30 o'clock, when the pursuit was suspended to rest the men and horses that had toiled in the mountains under a hot sun, without water. The general was satisfied. "No troops ever behaved better or in a more soldierly manner," he reported, remarking that the four or five-mile chase had "filled the forests of the Blue Mountains with fugitives." The troops lost five men wounded, one mortally. Bernard's charge in waves again had won a striking victory with small loss. He had not "hived" the Bannocks, as Howard desired, but he had struck and scattered them so that they no longer were a menace.

The fugitives tried to cross the Columbia River, but were turned back by gunboats under Captain John A. Kress of the Ordnance Department and ten men of that usually non-combatant branch of the service, and Lieutenant M. C. Wilkinson with ten men of the Twenty-first Infantry. Then Captain Miles' seven companies of the Twenty-first Infantry and two companies of the Fourth Artillery got their chance after their long march. They had been joined at the Umatilla Reservation by Company K of Bernard's battalion. The hostiles sought refuge and reinforcements here, being deceived by promises of the Umatillas, but were met by the troops instead, and again were defeated. Finding that army detachments were closing in on them from all sides, the Indians now started back along the way they had come.

Bernard's battalion, meanwhile, had been ordered to Fort Walla Walla, Washington, to refit. Here Lieutenant Colonel James W. Forsyth arrived fresh from General Sheridan's headquarters in Chicago, resplendent in correct uniform, in striking contrast to the sorry attire of the troopers who had been a month and a half on the trail. He assumed command of the battalion, which started out July 13th for Lewistown, on reports that the Indians were headed that way. But before it had gone very far, it was turned back on learning of the attack on Captain Miles at the reservation. Forsyth soon learned that Miles had been well able to take care of himself, so turned about again and took up the Bannock trail. On July 17th he came across a camp of Umatillas who had followed the retreating hostiles from the reservation, had attacked them, and killed Chief Egan, as proof of which they displayed his severed head and arm. For this victory, accomplished through treachery, the Umatillas got more credit than they deserved, for Egan probably was less blamable in the whole affair than Chief U-ma-pine of the Umatillas, who now appeared in the guise of a good friend of the whites.

Forsyth's command pushed forward through woods and swamps, and on July 20th struck the rear guard of the Bannocks in the canyon of the North Fork of John Day's River. "The canyon is twelve hundred feet deep, and as its walls are nearly perpendicular, my command literally slid down the trail that we were following and climbed up the opposite side," says Forsyth's description. The ascent was so steep that several pack animals fell over backward and were lost, and at the top of this gorge some forty Indians were seen. Eight civilian scouts were in advance of the troops; one of them accidentally discharged his gun, and the Indians fired, killing one, and wounding two.

Captain Winters with Company E, in advance, deployed, dismounted and took up a strong position. To his aid were sent Companies H under Lieutenant Parnell and L under Lieutenants E. H. Shelton, and W. C. Brown, while Colonel Bernard, again commanding his own troop, G, was sent up the side of the canyon to a projecting point which commanded and protected the trail. It took about an hour and a half for Bernard's troop to make this difficult climb, but when it reached the designated position the combination was unbeatable. The entire line charged, but the Indians were gone. The last stand of the Bannocks was a fizzle.

The Bannocks stampeded from this battlefield, so much so that the troops found evidences of the hurried flight all along the trail, the most remarkable of which was an Indian papoose, probably brushed from the back of a pack mule and not missed until it was too late. The papoose was turned over to the adjutant of the command, who got much solicited and unsolicited advice on the care and feeding of infants, but it survived a diet of ginger snaps and sugar, and when General Howard's headquarters arrived, was turned over to the care of Sarah Winnemucca and her sister-in-law. Sarah had continued on duty at headquarters throughout the campaign, and preferred to be as near as possible to Bernard's troop, where she had been treated with the respect she thought her due. She took care of the Indian baby until the war was over, and then took it about the various Indian camps until she found its parents, who had mourned it as dead.

At Stein's Mountains signal fires were seen, but Sarah soon proved these to be made by one lonesome Indian. The hostiles had scattered, and were drifting back to their reservations. It only remained to round up small parties still in the field. At Sinker's Mill on Sinker Creek, near Silver City, Idaho, Howard again was able to give Bernard a separate command, detaching him with

Companies D and G to gather up the Indians in Duck Valley and South Mountain. The remainder of Howard's force was scattered in similar small parties to complete the "hiving" as he called it, comparing the scattered Indians to a swarm of bees.

After scouting the country along the Nevada-Idaho line and paying a brief visit to Fort McDermit, Bernard returned with his troops to Boise Barracks August 29th, having marched since he left there May 30th a distance of one thousand and forty miles. It was a chase almost as long as that after Chief Joseph of the year before, but the results were far different. Not once had the troops suffered a defeat. Their losses were inconsiderable. The Indians had been pushed so hard and so rapidly that little opportunity was given them for rapine and plunder.

Bernard had given them their first two defeats, and was instrumental in driving them off in their final united action. In every move he had demonstrated the proper method of conducting Indian warfare.

His long delayed brevet as brigadier general finally came February 27, 1890, "for gallant service in action against Indians at Chiricahua Pass, Arizona, October 20, 1869, and in the actions against Indians near the Silver River, Oregon, June 23, 1878, and at Birch Creek, Oregon, July 8, 1878."

IX

THE SHEEPEATER CAMPAIGN*

IT was early in May of 1879. There was a hint of
spring in the air at Boise Barracks that was belied
by the heavy snow on the mountain tops to the
northward. But an unfailing sign of spring in that period
of the old west had arrived that moment from headquarters of the Department of the Columbia at Vancouver
Barracks.

"Well, Bernard, here are your orders for the summer
campaign," said Captain Collins who had summoned his
cavalry commander immediately upon the receipt of the
dispatch. "Five Chinamen killed by the Sheepeaters at
Oro Grande."

"I'll have the troop turned out at once."

"Oh, there's no hurry about it, Colonel. The killing
took place last February. And besides the order says you
are not to start before June 1st. This is one time you will
have to hold your horses, and I think I am going to enjoy
watching you get ready for an expedition in an orderly
and military manner, instead of dashing off and winning
the war before anyone else gets a chance, as you usually
do. But there's the order. Read it."

" 'Small band of Indians composed of Sheepeaters,
Piutes and Bannocks who escaped from the hostiles last
year—I thought they'd find some of the Bannocks got

---

*Bibliography: *The Sheepeater Campaign,* by W. C. Brown
(Idaho Historical Society, 1926) ; "We Never Forget," by W. C.
Brown in *The Quartermaster Review,* March-April, 1926; "The
Sheepeater Campaign," by C. B. Hardin in *Journal of the Mili-
tary Service Institution,* 1910; "The Sheepeater Campaign," by
C. B. Hardin and T. E. Wilcox in *Recreation,* June, 1907. Jour-
nals or diaries of E. F. Albrecht, R. F. Bernard, W. C. Brown,
John Corliss, Edgar Hoffner, Orlando Robbins, John Neville,
and L. A. Secor.

away in that direction—'located on the Middle Fork of the Salmon River'—I didn't know there was one. 'A force will be sent from Camp Howard . . . about fifty effectives. . . . The department commander desires that Captain Bernard be placed in command.' Well, now, that's right handsome of the general."

"That's not all. He really means it. Read on," Collins demanded. Bernard spelled out the order slowly and with some difficulty.

" '—And if he be not at the post by the time indicated for starting that these headquarters be notified by telegraph of the fact. It is expected that when the two commands come together Captain Bernard will be the ranking officer and the command of both forces will devolve upon him. This is the intention of the department commander.' Well—"

"It looks like your benefit, Bernard. By the way, I am making one change in your orders. You will go up Loon Creek instead of eastward to Challis. I've just had a report that two ranchers have been killed by the Indians at the South Fork of the Salmon. The place is called Johnson's Ranch and Hugh Johnson is one of the men reported killed. The other is his partner, Peter Dorsey. But I think you had better look in on the Chinamen first and see if you can pick up a trail there. Then you can work westward toward the force from Camp Howard, and visit Johnson's ranch on the way. I'll notify headquarters to that effect."

"I don't know much about the country."

"Neither does anyone else. Most of the maps we have leave middle Idaho a perfect blank. Here's a late government map that encloses the entire section you are going into with a dotted line and marks it 'UNEXPLORED.' We know a little more than that; that there are three forks of the Salmon River, that there is Loon Creek and a few more, but just how they run we're not sure. Rube Robbins knows a little about it, and there is a little Dutchman here, Johnny Vose, who claims to know all about it, and I will give him to you for what he is worth. The Fletcher map probably is the best, and between all of them I suspect you and Rube will have to follow your own ideas."

Company G, of course, was always ready, so it was especially well prepared on this occasion. Upon reading the order carefully, Bernard noted it said "on or about" June 1st, so, as might be expected, it was nine o'clock on the morning of May 31st that Tommy Fenton's trumpet sounded "Boots and Saddles," sending some sixty enlisted men on the backs of their California broncos, ready to go. A pack train in charge of ten civilian employees carried sixty days' rations for the command.

From the start the pack train was in trouble. The first day's march was thirty-five miles to Idaho City, even then an old placer mining town, six thousand feet in elevation. The pack train fell behind, and the men had very little to eat until it got in, after nine o'clock at night. The next day the march was forty miles down hill to the East Fork of the Payette River, and again the pack train did not get in until after nine. The third day the pack train suffered its first losses when mules were rolled over and over in the swift current of Hot or Warm Creek. The loss was only two boxes of hard bread, a sack of sugar, and a sack of salt, partly compensated for by Vose's luck in killing a deer. Another bad sign was the fact that snow two feet deep was encountered—on the second day of June.

The next day real troubles began. The troop entered Dead Man's Canyon, so called because two men had

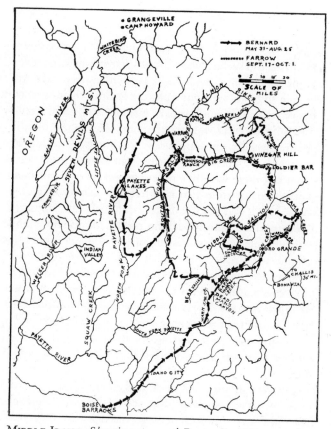

MIDDLE IDAHO. *Showing scene of Bernard's 1879 campaigns, his route from May 31st to the break-up of the expedition against the Sheepeaters, and the route of Lieutenants E. S. Farrow and W. C. Brown in their final drive from Rains' Ranch to the point where the Indians surrendered.*

(From map by Brigadier General W. C. Brown in his *The Sheepeater Campaign.*)

once been buried there by a snow slide. The steep sides of this canyon collected snow that seldom had a chance to melt—in some places it was found to be twenty feet deep. But the surface was so hard that it would bear the weight of a horse, and the cavalrymen were able to struggle through for eight miles by leading their mounts. "Every few minutes a horse, or a trooper, or both, would stand on their head, but would come up smiling, or the opposite, usually the opposite," Private Edgar Hoffner has recorded. Then after getting out of the snow, rain started and there were five miles of mud to be negotiated. Another extract from Private Hoffner's diary will give a view of the less enjoyable features of such campaigning. "I was troubled with an aching tooth," he records, "and having no dentist, I sat astride a log and pried out the offender with my pocket knife." Of course the pack train could not keep up. Fortunately Bernard had killed a deer that morning with the trumpeter's rifle, and Vose had killed another, so there was venison for dinner, but little was left for the evening meal.

June 4th was spent waiting for the pack train, and in building a bridge across Cape Horn Creek, so it could move on when it arrived. Meanwhile there was nothing to eat except grouse, fool hens, and ground squirrels. All day it rained and snowed. But at seven o'clock the pack train got in, to the great joy of everyone except Second Lieutenant John Pitcher. One of the mules had lost his footing in crossing a stream, and in order to save the animal, its pack had been cut loose. It happened to be the pack containing all of Lieutenant Pitcher's blankets and personal belongings. Of course he was ready to volunteer to go back next morning to help bring in the rest of the load. On the way he found his bundle caught in some driftwood, so he returned to camp happy again, with the pack train the next night. June 6th, next day, was spent in rest. The troopers had put up their shelter tents—even then called "pup tents"—and advantage was taken of the halt to have all the horses reshod. There was no rest for the troop blacksmith. The shoes were put on cold, but of course had been fitted previously, each soldier carrying a set of shoes for his own animal.

The marches became short, because of snow, rain, mud and difficulties with the pack train at every crossing of small, but swift, streams. Only ten miles was made June 7th and fourteen miles the following day. This was across the mountains in the snow, and Johnny Vose soon confessed himself lost.

"Why do you think you are lost?" asked Bernard, more amused than alarmed.

"Vel, me no see de trail; me no see any t'ings dat I knows; me no see de blazes on de trees," said the excited trailer.

"How do you expect to see a trail where the snow is ten or twelve feet deep?" Bernard inquired. "Do you think the blazes were cut in the tops of the trees? I don't think we are lost, for there is no other way to go. So don't worry about it."

But soon the snow became less deep, and Johnny was cheered by finding some of the blazes he had been look- ing for. That night the command camped on Loon Creek, and the next day reached Oro Grande, or Casto. This town in 1877 had enjoyed a considerable gold strike. Its placer mines had been worked for a long time, and a considerable village had grown up, but at last the claims were worked out and the miners had gone on to rosier- looking fields, selling out their holdings at a small price to Chinamen who were glad to go over them for smaller profits. This had been the history of mining in many

[139]

parts of the old west. In February the Chinamen had been killed and the town burned. It was never proved that this was done by Indians, and it is possible the Chinamen were killed for their gold by white robbers. It later was found that the Sheepeaters or Tukuarikas, a division of the Shoshoni, named for their living on the Rocky Mountain sheep, wintered at a spot that made it improbable that they had visited Oro Grande in February.

The town was not entirely abandoned in June. Three white men were found there, "waiting for something to turn up," says Bernard. In a garden, presumed to belong to one of the dead Chinamen, was a fine lot of green onions. "We threw out a skirmish line and charged," says Private Hoffner, "and in ten minutes there was not an onion left to tell the tale." But the tale was told, nevertheless. The next day there appeared a Chinaman from Bonanza City, thirty miles away, who stated with many protestations and much volubility that he was the rightful owner of the onion patch. His claim was allowed by Colonel Bernard and settled for twenty-five dollars, probably a cheap price for a gold region, and very likely a good investment for the prevention of scurvy among the troops. But the twenty-five dollar onions did not go very far, and within two days the troopers were again eating "scouse," a dish probably not described in the modern *Cooks' and Bakers' Manual*, but which consisted of stewed hard-tack and bacon fat. The hunters found a few deer, half-starved ground squirrels, wide-footed mountain rabbits, and fool hens to help out. The fool hen, identified as the Franklin grouse, is described by Bernard as a dark brown bird with red over each eye, so gentle as to be killed easily with a stick, and seldom frightened away even when sticks are thrown at it again and again.

[140]

"In ten minutes there was not an onion left to tell the tale."

While resting here Bernard sent to Bonanza for newspapers and to get information. Meanwhile he sent his pack train, unloaded, back to help a train that was bringing him additional supplies from Boise Barracks. By this time many of the packers were ready to quit. They had had quite enough of working in snow and rain. To add to their troubles, the streams were now rising so rapidly that it seemed to be impossible to cross them in the direction Bernard wanted to go. An attempt in another direction developed a rocky country impassable for animals, so much so that one of the horses of the scouting party was severely cut by a fall on the rocks. If this were not enough, both Lieutenant Pitcher and Rube Robbins were taken seriously ill with mountain fever. "I am the doctor," Bernard records, "and have nothing but cathartic and quinine pills to give them, while this and brandy is our supply of medicines—I wouldn't know how to use but very few other medicines if I had them."

So far, very little had been learned about the Indians. The reports of prospectors who had come into camp from Bonanza were vague. Later there arrived a prospector from the Yellow Jacket mining district who reported he had seen Indian signs on Camas Creek, some seventy miles away. "The man has a rifle and eighteen cartridges, two blankets and about thirty pounds of flour, and says he has eaten nothing but bread and salt, with an occasional grouse, for six months," Bernard records. "He is looking well, is cheerful, ragged and dirty. So we will march in the morning and go to the place where the man says he saw the Indian signs though I don't believe his story at all."

Lieutenant Pitcher, having recovered, undertook the bridging of Loon Creek. His solution of this engineering problem was to drop a tree across it, but several trees broke in falling and were carried away. At last one was dropped to span the stream. By that time the day was spent and next morning it was found that the water had fallen sufficiently to permit the animals to cross, so the bridge was not completed. At about this time John S. Ramey, an experienced guide, had joined, being sent from department headquarters. After leaving Loon Creek, the command followed a second Hot Creek, or Warm Creek, which had to be crossed several times with a net loss of two mules and four packs. The hot springs along this stream, however, provided warm baths that were much appreciated by the men as they made camp after a march of eighteen miles.

The West Fork of Camas Creek was reached on June 21st and all was made ready for an attack on the Indian camp reported there. Soon fresh pony tracks were seen. The command was halted, cinches tightened, the troopers remounted and a charge was ordered. As the gorge opened out into a wide flat, smoke was seen up the canyon and horses grazing in the valley. The troops galloped until the horses were passed and then Bernard brought the command to a walk to align his force for the final charge. As he did so he saw three miners with rifles running for the rocks at the side of the canyon. It was the smoke of their fires that had been seen by the owner of the eighteen cartridges. The miners, when assured that they were not being charged by Indians, reported that they had spent the winter along Camas Creek and had seen no signs of the Sheepeaters.

For the next few days the march was continued under the usual adverse conditions—rain, snow, mud, and, as an additional feature, a hail storm with hailstones as large as pigeon eggs reported. If this seems large consider the estimates of a few men hit by them, who said the hailstones were as large as water buckets. In crossing one mountain a mule tumbled and rolled from top to bottom, a distance of six hundred yards, and was reported dead. He came limping into camp the next day, considerably bruised, but able to continue the journey. At last the mountains were crossed and the valley of the Middle Salmon River reached in a rapid descent—"within a distance of ten miles," says Bernard, "we have come from ten feet of snow to roses and rattlesnakes." The presence of the rattlesnakes was impressed on his mind by finding one about sixteen inches long, coiled in his blankets one morning. "As the morning was quite cold," Bernard remarks, "the snake was very inactive. He was gently laid in a camp fire to get warm."

The valley of the Middle Salmon had never been followed by anyone, according to Ramey. It had been tried in the winter on the ice, but there were too many rapids and waterfalls. For the most part it ran through a gorge

One mule holding on (with its teeth) until it could be pulled out.

with perpendicular banks, reaching up into the mountain ranges on either side. This was the trail Bernard now attempted. Trouble started at the crossing of Loon Creek near its mouth. A bridge was constructed for the men, but it was not suitable for the animals. In swimming the mules across many were carried far down stream. One mule displayed remarkable intelligence in seizing a strong willow bush with its teeth and holding on until it could be pulled out with ropes. When rescued it was given three hearty cheers by the men. But two thousand cartridges, two hundred pounds of horseshoes, a box of hard-tack, three sides of bacon and a pack saddle were lost, and to add to Bernard's gloom, when he went hunting he killed only five grouse "and got a shot at a deer, and should have been kicked for not killing it," as he records disgustedly. During the next five days trail was made with pick and shovel during the day, and in the evening an officer and a guide would scout the country ahead to see if further progress was possible. This slow progress was continued at the rate of ten to eighteen miles a day for a total of seventy miles.

On the first of July the command was halted at Rapid River, a narrow torrent that it was necessary to bridge. A large tree was dropped across the stream, and small logs lashed on either side, on the top of which branches were laid and leaves and earth spread. The animals took to this bridge more readily than had been expected, but, needless to say, none of the men attempted it mounted. After the command had entirely crossed, the bridge was dismantled to recover the ropes used as lashings, leaving only the single log, and there was much speculation as to the amazement of anyone coming along in time to see the trail of a company of cavalry and its pack train leading down to and away from a single log. It would appear that all of the horses and mules were accomplished tight-rope walkers.

The next day the trail was so steep that eight mules fell and rolled into the river, six of them swimming to the opposite side, and two others being drowned. Lieutenant Pitcher swam his horse across the stream—again it was his baggage that was in trouble — and with the aid of the chief packer, Jake Barnes, recovered the six mules. Three packs were lost in this accident, and all the sugar and salt washed away. The losses were rapidly becoming so heavy as to endanger the success of the expedition. Fortunately game was plentiful—mountain sheep, deer and bear were found. That a famous scout may occasionally miss a shot is recorded in this connection, for Bernard notes that, "Robbins met a black bear and shot at it, but did not kill it. Some of the men asked him if he only tried to scare it away, as it was but about fifty yards from him. This seemed to plague Robbins very much, as he prides himself on being a good shot."

There were other bear stories. Major Hardin tells of a man he refuses to identify further than as "Reddy," whose boast was that he had discovered a certain method of disposing of a wounded bear. He would lie on his back, so he said, and allow the bear to walk over him, whereupon with a swift upward motion of a very sharp knife he would deprive the bear of large sections of its vital organs. Naturally his companions were eager to see this method demonstrated and hoped to find a sufficiently angry wounded bear to be worth Reddy's attention. At last the chance came. A bear was wounded. They followed the trail of blood. "The more blood Reddy saw, the braver he became," says Major Hardin. "He was soon quite a warrior, taking the lead, partly through his own bravery, but chiefly through our courtesy." But when the bear was found, it was much alive and quite active. For some reason Reddy did not try his superior method, but instead ran briskly to take refuge on top of a tall rock, definitely refusing to demonstrate. The bear obligingly turned attention to Reddy's companions, and a few more shots ended the animal's career.

After July 2d the canon closed in, and further progress along the stream became impossible. The command was forced into the mountains and turned back eastward toward the old trail. The 4th of July was spent at a sulphur spring at the headwaters of Rapid River—or Crooked River, as Bernard calls it at this point—used as a lick by elk, moose, deer and Rocky Mountain sheep to so large an extent that for a mile from the spring the ground was described as cut up like a barnyard. The next day the old trail was reached, about six miles south of Oro Grande. At the Cape Horn River, near the point where the command had waited so long for the pack train in June, a halt of twelve days was made, while the train was sent into Boise Barracks to replenish supplies.

"We have traveled over much country that no white

A large tree was dropped across the stream.

man ever saw before, our guides and all miners declaring we could not get through at all," Bernard reported at this time, adding optimistically, "All streams are now falling fast, so I hope to get along with less trouble and less loss of rations than heretofore."

This optimism was justified, at least for the time being, and in the next stage of the campaign Bernard moved more rapidly and with little loss of rations. Up to this point he had scouted thoroughly the country east of the Middle Fork of the Salmon River, but had been unable to cross that stream and had turned back toward its headwaters. He now crossed over to the headwaters of the South Fork and moved down it to the main Salmon River. The Johnson Ranch, where two men had been killed by Indians, was reached July 29th. This part of the trip had not been without incident—there was still much snow, mud and rocks, but these presented little difficulty. Bear, deer, salmon and trout varied the menu, although the pack train was not losing quite so many sides of bacon and boxes of hard-tack. To give some further idea of how the troopers fared, Private Hoffner's recipe for baking bread may be cited. He had obtained some flour, with which he kneaded his dough on a rubber poncho. "Then dug a hole in the ground large enough for a mess pan about ten inches in diameter, then put in hot coals and heated hole, then placed dough on a tin pan, turning mess pan over it, placing coals over all and baked till done. We had salt and baking powder. The baking was a success. We then made gravy of flour, water and bacon grease. With venison steak and coffee we had a fine supper."

So far Bernard had received little information from the other forces in the field that were supposed to come under his command. One of these, under Lieutenant Henry Catley, had started from Camp Howard, north of the Salmon River, June 4th and had moved by way of Warren's and Rains' Ranch to Big Creek, between the two forks of the Salmon that Bernard had scouted. Catley had with him Lieutenants E. K. Webster and W. C. Muhlenberg and Company C and a detachment of Company K of the Second Infantry.

The other was a force of twenty Umatilla Indian scouts from their reservation in Oregon. It was led by Lieutenants Edward S. Farrow and W. C. Brown, and included seven enlisted men of Farrow's regiment, the Twenty-first Infantry, and a small pack train with a half dozen civilian packers. Farrow now reported that he had moved eastward as far as Payette River, but had turned westward on a report that the Sheepeaters were in the vicinity of Crooked River. Bernard received this report July 29th, and considering that Catley had a sufficient force to take care of himself operating in the only other section of the country where the Indians were likely to

be found, decided that his best move would be to support Farrow's small command which, it seemed most
likely, was following the main band of the Indians. Accordingly he moved out toward Warren's Diggins, since
known as Warren, which at this time consisted of a hotel,
a blacksmith shop, two or three general merchandise
stores, two saloons and about two dozen dwellings, and
was connected with the outside world only by a trail.
Earlier in the day the troops had feasted their eyes on the
spectacle of a Bannock squaw, wife of a white man, the
first woman they had seen in two months. But at Warren's the gentler sex was more adequately represented by
one white woman and one Chinese woman. Civilization
was soon left behind, however, and the march was continued until August 4th, seventy miles in the wrong
direction, as it proved. For it was now learned that Farrow had been following a false report much like that
investigated by Bernard early in the campaign. The
camp, supposedly of hostiles, proved to be only a party of
miners, and while Bernard was on this wild goose chase,
it was Catley who was in sad need of assistance.

For Catley had really found the Sheepeaters. While
following an Indian trail his command was ambushed
by hostiles concealed behind a wall they had built of
loose rock. Two men were wounded and the lieutenant
ordered a retreat. Within about two miles he met his
pack train and went into camp. The next morning, July
30th, the retreat was continued, but the Indians, actually
numbering twenty-seven at the highest estimate, seemed
to be on all sides of them, so the troops took refuge on
an eminence afterward known as Vinegar Hill for the
reason that the troops lacked water, so drank vinegar
from the provisions. The Indians set fire to the grass but
Catley's men were able to save themselves by counter-

[149]

firing. That night they retreated, abandoning most of their baggage. By this time the force was considerably demoralized and was headed back to Camp Howard by the shortest route until halted by peremptory orders to await the arrival of Bernard and of Captain A. G. Forse who was ordered out as a reinforcement with twenty-five men of Company D, First Cavalry.

Meanwhile the Indians attacked Rains' ranch, killing the owner, James Rains, and wounding Albert Webber.

Bernard hurried back from his wild goose chase, being joined on the way by Farrow's party August 6th, by Catley's company August 11th, and by Forse's troop August 12th. With these accessions he had a total of one hundred and seventy-eight officers and men, including scouts, guides, twenty Indians and twenty-two civilian packers. The next day he started a most difficult march. So steep is the canyon of Big Creek that at some points sunset came at two o'clock in the afternoon, according to reports. It is so narrow that often it was necessary to march for considerable distances in the water, where sharp rocks crippled the animals. The ponies of the Indian scouts, not being shod, suffered severely. Their hoofs were softened in the creek and the hard lava rock wore them down to the quick, with the result that half of them gave out and had to be shot to prevent their falling into the hands of the enemy. Many crossings of the creek were necessary—Private Hoffner records three on August 16th, ten on August 17th, seven on August 18th, and thirteen on August 19th. On this last day Farrow's scouts discovered the Sheepeaters, attacked them and pursued them several miles, capturing their camp and recovering a large part of the supplies they had taken from Catley's command. Bernard closely supported the scouts, but the hostiles kept moving and no general fight occurred.

The next day Bernard decided to send Catley's company back along the trail to meet an expected supply train, as rations were badly needed. At the same time he intended to continue the pursuit with the rest of the command. So at sunrise the infantrymen started on the back trail, while Troops D and G started the ascent of a very precipitous slope, leaving behind the two pack trains under a small guard, which were to follow as soon as made ready. Farrow's scouts had gone ahead as advance guard.

Bernard had been gone scarcely an hour when a sound of heavy firing was heard from the camp, the discharge of the carbines sounding almost as loud as artillery in the narrow canyon. Immediately Lieutenant Pitcher turned his horse around and started for the scene.

"Hold on, Mr. Pitcher," Bernard shouted. "Deploy as skirmishers and take it easy. We might catch something on the way down."

"But they might get the pack train," the lieutenant urged.

"Not by a damned sight," Bernard answered. "They've got a bear by the tail. I have men down there. Don't you hear the carbines?"

Bernard did have men there. It was only seven of them, but five were men of Troop G, which made a difference.

At the first fire from the hidden Indians, Private Harry Eagan of Company C, Second Infantry was mortally wounded, shot through both thighs. Before there was time for another volley, the sergeant and pack train guard from the Second Infantry had faded out of the picture. This left the fight up to Corporal Charles B. Hardin and his six troopers, two of D and four of G of the First Cavalry. Quickly they moved to a flanking position up the mountain. In this movement they had one ally, Jake Barnes, the chief packer, who moved his one hundred and twenty-five mules to a sheltered place, then picked up a rifle that had been dropped by one of the fleeing infantrymen and joined the corporal with the remark, "I want some of this myself. Private Barnes reports for duty, sir." This assistance from a noncombatant civilian employee cheered the men tremendously. The Indians, numbering about ten to fifteen, were driven off before Bernard returned. The courageous "little Dutchman" Johnny Vose was first of the relieving force to join the pack train guard.

Private Eagan had been carried out of danger, but was very seriously injured. The surgeon, T. E. Wilcox, who had quite an adventurous service on this campaign, attempted to amputate a leg, but Eagan died during the operation. He was buried on the spot. In 1925 the cemeterial division of the Quartermaster Corps, assisted by his regiment, erected a small monument to mark his grave, and so isolated is the region even today that the headstone was transported from the nearest railroad station seventy miles by wagon and nearly forty miles by pack mule.

The next day the two commands started out again, Bernard catching up with Farrow's scouts that night. Farrow had continued to push the Sheepeaters and had captured much of their supplies and some thirty abandoned horses and mules. The Indians had killed two horses and one mule for food. But Bernard's force by this time was almost as bad off, so he now issued what rations he had to Farrow, retaining only enough to last the two troops until they could reach Loon Creek where he expected to meet a pack train. In this he was disappointed, so he turned Forse's company back in the hope that it could get enough from Farrow to reach Catley with the expected supply train. But supplies failed on all sides. Farrow already was headed back, the supply train failed to meet Catley, and Forse had a starvation march back to Rains' Ranch. When Bernard reported the condition of his troop he was authorized to return to Boise Barracks to refit. He reached there September 8th.

So far the campaign had failed in its main object of rounding up the troublesome Indians, and with all of the troops returning to their stations there seemed no hope of accomplishing it. But Lieutenants Farrow and Brown determined on one more effort with their Umatilla Scouts. They rounded up an insufficient pack train and left Rains' Ranch September 17th with a total of twenty-three men, including packers. South of the Salmon and west of the Middle Fork they captured two squaws, a papoose and a boy. A few days later the infant Sheep-eater became honored on the map of Idaho by the name Papoose Gulch, which recalls the fact that he cried all night to the discomfort of the command while his mother tried unsuccessfully to get in touch with the hostiles with overtures for a surrender. After several negotiations fifty-one members of the band surrendered early in October. This ended the career of the Sheepeaters.

An off-hand judgment might find that Bernard had failed to accomplish anything and that Lieutenants Farrow and Brown with their scouts had brought the campaign to a successful conclusion by persuading the hostiles to surrender. Bernard's company had marched one thousand, one hundred and sixty-eight miles and the only fight to its credit was that of five of its enlisted men on Soldier's Bar of Big Creek. It had lost forty-five mules, eighteen horses and an immense amount of supplies. It then returned to its home station in a crippled condition.

But without detracting from the credit due to the two second lieutenants and their command, a service later given recognition by the brevet commissions of first lieutenant voted to Farrow and Brown and the naming of a peak in Papoose Gulch "Farrow Mountain," it may be pointed out that they did not surround the Sheepeaters and force a surrender. Very skillfully the two young officers negotiated with the hostile band and persuaded its leaders, discouraged by the unflagging pursuit by men of their own race, to give up the fight. But the Sheepeaters were ready to quit because of the demoralizing effect of that relentless drive led by Bernard down Big Creek, a pursuit pushed so vigorously that for once the Indians suffered even more than the troops. Their camps were destroyed wherever found, and they were reduced from faring on the Rocky Mountain sheep that had given them their name to horse steak and mule roast. Farrow's scouts were the spearhead of that drive, and had most of the fighting, but the consistent and close support of Bernard and the two troops of the First Cavalry in rear kept the Indians on the run. Bernard would have liked nothing better than to have them make a stand so he could get at them. Only once did they succeed in doubling back, and then they got so warm a reception from the small guard of Bernard's men that they did not attempt it again.

That Farrow and Brown had the courage and capability of making a final effort brought them deserved success. But Bernard's masterly movement, following upon a defeat for the troops, was the factor that made the surrender possible. And so far was Bernard's troop from being used up that even then it was again in the field.

Only eleven days after the arrival of Troop G at Boise Barracks it was ordered out again, on a report that In-

[154]

dians had raided in the valley of Squaw Creek, a branch of the Payette River. This locality was south and west of any of the territory scouted over previously during the summer. The report arrived at 8:00 A.M., September 19th, and the troop was on the road by 9:00, and that night was at the scene of action, having marched fifty miles.

Private Hoffner, who had been in Bernard's troop many years, was very skeptical of this Indian raid. Perhaps he was disgruntled at being routed out again, just after having been comfortably settled down for the winter, but he seems to take the whole story with more than a grain of salt. "We came to a flat," he says, "where we were told by the guide a party of citizens had a fight with the Indians. We found a carcass of beef, or part of it, that the so-called Indians had killed. . . . My private opinion is that the party was whites, as they had left too much of the beef behind them for Indians, and they had cleaned the tripe, and took the tongue, and took off the hide as a civilized person would do. . . . My opinion is that citizens of the valley, having grain and hay to dispose of and no market near, hit on this plan to make a few dimes. We have only a man's word, one we know nothing of, that a boy was wounded. . . . We failed to see the boy, or any indication of where the party was. There are several old Indian fighters in Troop G, Colonel Bernard and self included. We found no trail."

Nevertheless they marched over mountains and valleys to the northward, with no indication of doubt that they were trailing a band of marauders. It has been noticed before that Bernard did not hesitate to investigate any rumor, however much he doubted its truth, if there was nothing better to do. But his move to the northward, to the sites of camps of the summer campaign, suggests that he had in mind Farrow's scouts still operating in that region. Miners in the vicinity of Payette Lake reported they had seen no sign of Indians.

At one ranch the troopers were charged seventy-five cents for a dozen eggs, or a pound of butter or a gallon of milk. Private Hoffner was so ungrateful as to wish this rancher a few nights of nightmare and to express pity that no soap could be raised, as "his wife and children seem entire strangers to that useful commodity." But in contrast, at Solon Hall's ranch in Indian Valley, the soldiers found a beef dressed for them when they arrived, and they were told to help themselves to potatoes, cabbages and onions in the garden.

While in the mountains Bernard's horse fell over a bank, breaking its neck, which probably added little to his cheer when he found that this last expedition was destined to accomplish nothing. Farrow, by this time, was making his final roundup of the Sheepeaters far to the east. Bernard's troop ended its useless march October 5th.

The troop remained at Boise Barracks during the winter. In April it changed station to Fort McDermit, Nevada.

X

THE CHASE OF THE CHIRICAHUAS*

THE SHEEPEATER CAMPAIGN, arduous as it had been, added no battle, fight or "scrimmage" to Bernard's list, which had reached No. 101 at the close of the Bannock War in 1878 and was not to be completed by Numbers 102 and 103 until 1881 in the familiar field of Arizona.

The year 1880 was passed very quietly at the desolate post of Fort McDermit. On Christmas Day, in this isolated spot, was born his seventh child, Thomas Pitcher Bernard, now a colonel of Field Artillery. The middle name honored the second lieutenant who had proved so able an officer in Idaho and Oregon.

An unimportant scout of two hundred and twenty miles was made by Company G in July of 1881. All was quiet in the northwest, and it seemed that the usual summer campaign was over. But far away in Arizona the Apaches were stirring. A medicine man of the White Mountain sub-tribe was causing trouble near Fort Apache. An attempt to arrest him August 30th resulted in an uprising of the White Mountain Apaches and a mutiny of Indian Scouts. Captain Edmund C. Hentig of the Sixth Cavalry and several of his men were killed. Brevet Major General O. B. Willcox, commanding the department, felt that he had no troops that could be spared from garrisons to send to the scene of the Cibicu

---

*BIBLIOGRAPHY: "A Cavalry Horse of Ye Olden Days," by C. B. Hardin in *Winners of the West,* June 30, 1933; *Geronimo's Story of His Life,* taken down and edited by S. M. Barrett (New York, 1906); *The Truth About Geronimo,* by Britton Davis (New Haven, 1929); *Lieutenant Charles B. Gatewood and the Surrender of Geronimo,* by Maj. C. B. Gatewood, Order of Indian Wars of the United States, Jan. 26, 1929; *Trailing Geronimo,* by Anton Mazzanovich (Los Angeles, 1926).

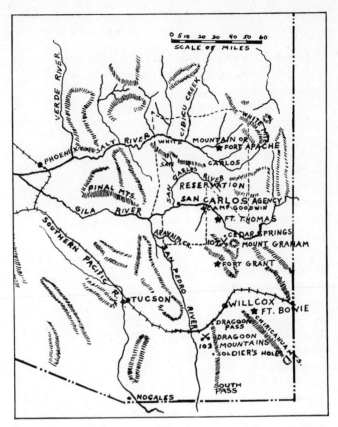

SOUTHEASTERN ARIZONA. *Showing scene of Bernard's 1881
campaign and locations of his fights Nos. 102 and 103.*
(Based on contemporary maps.)

battle. He asked that assistance be sent from neighboring commands.

There were a large number of companies within a radius of one thousand miles from the San Carlos Reservation. Few of them were especially busy. But from them all the troop of Colonel Bernard, far north in Nevada, almost on the Idaho line, was selected. Perhaps it was thought that he would get there first.

On the morning of September 4th, five days after the killing of Captain Hentig, Corporal Luther A. Secor, later Bernard's first sergeant, was on herd guard in a canyon north of Fort McDermit. At noon he sent two men into the post for dinner. They came galloping back with orders to bring in the stock and get ready to move. When the animals arrived the troopers were ready to saddle up, and within a half hour the company was on its way without waiting for rations or transportation. All that afternoon and far into the night they rode, to within twelve miles of Winnemucca. As usual Bernard was a bit too precipitate for the somewhat orderly army manner of doing things "immediately." The railway cars that were to carry the troop to "somewhere in Arizona" would not arrive until the following afternoon. The next day the eighty mile march was completed, the troopers were given a meal at a hotel, the animals were loaded and the company sat down to await the arrival of Company I. In the course of the afternoon Company I's train arrived, and the two troops were on their way, down through Nevada and California and into Arizona, by way of Truckee, Sacramento, and Lathrop. Troops moving by railroad were no common sight during the Indian wars, but Bernard was to prove the value of speedy transportation even further before the campaign was over.

On the fourth day the two troops arrived at Willcox, Arizona, and unloaded. Wagons, mule teams and travel rations had been picked up along the way. That afternoon they marched to Fort Grant, the next day to Fort Thomas, and the third day to San Carlos Agency, where the trouble centered. A pack train was acquired here, and within two weeks of receiving orders in far off Nevada they were scouting in the White Mountains of Arizona. Within a few days they ran into the band of Indians who were the objects of this long chase. Thirty warriors, with a number of women, surrendered without a fight. The prisoners were taken to San Carlos, placed in wagons in irons, and started for Willcox with the two troops, under Major George B. Sanford, as escort.

On the first day of October they marched to Fort Thomas. On the next day, while on the way to Fort Grant, a courier overtook them about four miles from Cedar Springs, near Mount Graham, with information that three hundred Apaches had left the San Carlos Agency with the intention of rescuing the prisoners.

This band proved to be Chiricahua Apaches, who had killed Chief Sterling of the agency police at Camp Goodwin, and were now definitely on the war path. Their hereditary chief was Nahche—also written Nachez and Nachite—who was the son of Cochise, Bernard's enemy of 1869 and 1870. But Nahche had little of the ability of his father, and another chief, Juh, disputed the leadership. A rival of Juh at this time, later to become the last of the famous Indian chiefs, was a warrior of less than sub-chief's rank, who by sheer courage and determination dominated the history of the Apache Wars. He was Geronimo, at this time notable only because of an arrest for murder in 1877 and subsequent escape on a raiding expedition into Mexico. But already in 1881 he was disputing the leadership with Juh, and had a following of a considerable number of Chiricahuas. The reason for the outbreak of October, 1881, is given by General Willcox as the refusal of the agent to help Juh and Nahche in constructing an irrigation ditch. Geronimo probably was not much interested in that problem. He was interested in maintaining his independence of Juh, so kept "Geronimo's band" on the reservation—for the time being.

Shortly after the courier delivered his message, the two troops of the First Cavalry sighted the Chiricahuas. The wagons were formed in two lines, with the cavalry horses, in charge of the Number Fours, in between the two lines, while the dismounted troopers formed skirmish lines around the wagon train. In this formation the Apaches were held at a safe distance for about an hour, when Companies A and F of the Sixth Cavalry, under Lieutenants G. E. Overton and J. N. Glass arrived to help out. Overton's company deployed, dismounted, as soon as it came under fire, and Bernard now mounted his troop and charged. As soon as the two companies made a junction, the Apaches began to leave, but Bernard continued after them into the hills. There, at about 8 o'clock, the Indians made a determined effort to drive Bernard back, firing seven volleys and approaching within ten feet of his men—unusually close for Apache warfare, for these Indians were more notable in ambush than in charges. But Company G held its ground and drove the Apaches back, returning to the wagons only when darkness made it impossible to see anything of the hostiles. In this fight of October 2d a sergeant of Company F of the Sixth Cavalry was killed. Two of Bernard's men were wounded.

Fort Grant was reached that night. The next morn-

"Then, advancing at a gallop, we commenced firing."

ing the two troops of the Sixth Cavalry took up the pursuit of the Indians, while the two of the First took the prisoners to Willcox and turned them over to a company of Infantry there. In the afternoon the troops of the Sixth came in to report that the Indians were headed for the Dragoon Mountains, a range running north and south not far from the Mexican line. That night Companies F and H of the Ninth Cavalry, a colored organization then, as it is now, arrived at Willcox by train from Texas.

The morning of October 4th a dramatic chase began. Colonel Bernard was given command of the six troops from three regiments. His first act was to commandeer a railroad train for the chase—a most original idea in Indian warfare. The horses and pack mules were loaded into box cars, but most of the men clung to the tops of the cars. After several miles of this precarious and comfortable transportation, the Indians were sighted crossing the track some four or five miles ahead, near the Dragoon Pass. Gallantly the puffing little wide-funneled locomotive speeded for the spot and stopped. Doors of the box cars were lifted off their hangers and used for gangways, the horses were hastily unloaded, and the men mounted, and were off in pursuit.

"We formed left front into line, with two-yard intervals, First Cavalry on the right, Sixth on the left, and Ninth in center," says Sergeant Secor. "Then, advancing at a gallop, we commenced firing. The Indians would make a stand on every high elevation, trying to hold us in check. This they did to some extent, but we would soon outflank them, and then they would beat it. This was kept up for from twenty to twenty-five miles. Then they turned into the mountains, at a very bad, rocky place, and we had to dismount to fight on foot."

The horses and pack mules were loaded into box cars.

At this point some twenty or thirty of the Apaches were separated from the main body, and against these Lieutenant Pitcher charged with a platoon of about twenty men from Troop G, and drove this band into the mountains. But as soon as the Apaches reached the rocks they were able to take positions from which they could hold the troopers at bay. Soon after dark Bernard took Troop G on a roundabout course of about five miles through a pass, in an attempt to cut off the Indians, but his troop arrived too late. Already the Chiricahuas had escaped.

The next morning Bernard continued the pursuit, sending back word from Soldier's Hole at the south end of the Dragoon Mountains that the Apaches apparently were headed for Mexico and that he would follow them if he did not receive orders to the contrary. At this time there existed an agreement with Mexico permitting troops of either nationality to cross the international boundary after hostile bands under certain conditions, but it never was entirely clear just what those conditions were, and such invasions on the part of United States troops usually brought forth some objection from Mexico. General Willcox referred Bernard's communication through military channels, and presumably it eventually was referred by the War Department to the State Department, and what happened to it after that General Willcox did not know at the time he made his annual report for that year to the War Department. Meanwhile, of course, Bernard's command invaded Mexico, and, in fact was on its way back because of lack of rations when orders finally reached the colonel for his return.

Juh and Nahche had visited the mountains of Chihuahua before and were out of sight soon after Bernard crossed the border. The six troops had very few provisions when they started out, and these were soon exhausted, so Bernard was forced to give up the chase. Juh had a small personal celebration in honor of his escape, and while drunk fell into a river and was drowned. In April, 1822, Geronimo led out his small band and joined Nahche. They were persuaded to return to the reservation two years later, Geronimo bringing with him a large herd of cattle that he had collected from Mexican ranches. The United States paid the looted Mexicans for Geronimo's cattle, and then confiscated the herd for the use of the reservation. This was one of the causes for Geronimo's final and most famous outbreak, when five thousand regular troops were used in the effort to run down his small band.

But Bernard had completed his one hundred and three battles with the affair at the South Pass of the Dragoon Mountains, October 4, 1881. After the return of the troop from Mexico—and from this time it was reported officially as a "Troop" and not a "Company" although general orders to this effect were not issued until 1883 —it was stationed for a time at its old post of Fort Bowie, and then went back, in November, to Fort Mc-

Dermit. The following spring it returned to another familiar post, Fort Bidwell.

Here, November 1, 1882, Bernard ended his career in the First Cavalry. On this date he was promoted to be major in the Eighth Cavalry. For twenty-seven years he had been in the same regiment, in every grade from recruit and blacksmith to captain and brevet colonel. For fourteen years he had commanded Company G; for sixteen years he had been a captain.

The Indian wars were drawing near their close. In the decade from 1880 to 1890 there was a sharp drop in the number of skirmishes and expeditions. Geronimo was carrying on the campaign that made him the last of famous Indian chiefs, and Sitting Bull of the Sioux was to meet death in one final outbreak to the north. But settlement was rapidly closing in and in 1890 the "Frontier Line" disappeared from the maps. But this decade was the flower of the range cattle industry when the wild west of the cowboy was stamping itself upon the national consciousness, to be subject matter for thousands of novels, short stories, plays and motion pictures. Abilene, Tombstone and Deadwood and a hundred more had their day of shootings and cussedness, bringing to the fore the names of "Wild Bill" Hickok, Wyatt Earp, "Calamity Jane" and a host of other frontier characters.

Laredo, Texas, also had its day of wild and woolly west-ness, and its day was election day in 1886. Local political parties styling themselves "Botas" and "Guaraches" had worked up a bitter feud and there was every indication of bloodshed before the day was over. As was not unusual in the West, sheriff and city marshal headed the opposing factions. As early as 7:30 in the morning sounds arose from downtown Laredo that resembled an old-fashioned Fourth of July celebration. But the noise came not from firecrackers, but from pistols.

Fort McIntosh, nearby, was commanded by Major Reuben F. Bernard of the Eighth Cavalry, who had as garrison Troop A of his regiment and Companies D and E of the Sixteenth Infantry. There was no occasion for him to leave the confines of the military reservation. If he did intervene there was very little chance that he would get any thanks for it from anyone, and a very strong possibility that he would face a court martial for an unwarranted invasion of the rights of citizens without authority.

But Bernard could not be kept out of a fight, if he thought there was any possibility of his doing it any good. Legalistic arguments had no appeal for him. Here was something going on that he thought he should stop. To his mind it was the primary duty of the army to preserve the peace.

When the firing started, an officer was sent to the town to find out what was going on. The officer returned and reported that there was firing from house tops and from around corners on everyone that appeared in the streets, and that some twenty persons had been killed. Bernard had "To Arms" sounded, calling out his garrison. Then it was reported to him that armed parties from Mexico were crossing the Rio Grande river into the town to take part in the fight.

"That's what I've been waiting for," he exclaimed. "Now we'll go in and stop it."

He ordered his Cavalry troop to remain under arms near the reservation gate, to be ready to move when ordered. He then formed his two companies of Infantry in column of fours, and led them into the town. Without looking to the right or left he marched his command

[167]

down the street along which most of the fighting was going on. As the troops appeared the fighting stopped, to be resumed again as soon as they had passed. The Infantry paid no attention to this, but continued the march until the city hall was reached. There it was halted.

Bernard then sent for the sheriff and the city marshal and informed them that he had taken charge of the town. All firing must cease immediately, and all firearms must be brought to the city hall and surrendered to the troops. The leaders of both factions agreed to this program. An army ambulance was soon filled with pistols, shotguns, rifles and other arms. Patrols were sent out and all citizens appearing on the streets were searched for arms. All saloons were arbitrarily closed. Sentries were posted at the post office, custom house and banks. After noon business houses began to re-open, reassured by the constant patrolling of the streets by squads of soldiers. Orders were issued that no one was to appear on the streets after dark unless supplied with a pass signed by military authorities. Patrols enforced these orders during the night.

Now came the time for explanations. With no authority from anyone Bernard had invaded a city and declared martial law. He reported his action by telegraph to to adjutant general of the department at San Antonio, setting forth that there was no civil authority to take charge and stop the riot, since city and county authorities were opposing each other, that armed parties from Mexico were joining in the fighting, and that the custom house and post office were exposed to looting. There had been no time to inform department headquarters or await orders.

However there were no complaints from any quarter. Both political parties agreed in thanking Bernard for his

Lieutenant Colonel Reuben F. Bernard, 9th Cavalry.
Taken about 1892.

prompt action. Citizens were grateful. The state had no complaint. From army superiors came nothing but praise and general orders of the army mentioned among those who distinguished themselves by especially meritorious acts or conduct, Major Bernard "for the promptness and discretion with which he suppressed a dangerous riot in Laredo, Texas."* Rare judgment must have been exemplified to meet such universal commendation.

Bernard received his long delayed brevet as brigadier general in 1890. Two years later he was promoted lieutenant colonel of the Ninth Cavalry. He retired October 14, 1896. His wife died in 1891. He was married a second time, after a year's interval, to Ruth Lavinia Simpson at Baltimore, Maryland. She died within a year, shortly after giving birth to a son, Robert Simpson Bernard now resident of Baltimore. General Bernard was married a third time, shortly after his retirement, to Elzie May Camp at Knoxville, Tennessee, his boyhood home.

General Bernard was Deputy Governor of the Soldiers' Home at Washington, D. C. from 1896 until shortly before his death. He was first president of the Order of Indian Wars and retained that office six years. He died November 17, 1903.

With his death there passed a master of minor warfare. For leadership in the troop or battalion operations that were characteristic of the campaigns against the Indians, he was one of the most efficient Cavalry officers carried on the rolls of the army during his long period of gallant and arduous service. In the larger field of generalship he was untested. But as captain of a troop in active campaign he ranked not far from first.

---

*G.O. No. 39, Hq., Army, A.G.O., Apr. 9, 1891.

THE END

APPENDIX

Numerical and Chronological List of General Bernard's Fights and Scrimmages.

New Mexico	1856
1. Headwater of Gila River	March 28
(D, 1st Cavalry)	
2. On the Mimbres River	April 5
Arizona	1858
3. In Pinal Mountains	December 25
4. San Carlos River	December 27
5. Pinal Mountains	December 30
	1859
6. On San Pedro River	November 9
	1860
7. Near Fort Buchanan	January 20
	1861
8. San Carlos River	January 21
New Mexico	1862
9. Near Fort Craig	February 19
10. Valverde	February 21
11. In mountains near Socorro	February 26
12. Apache Canon	March 28
13. Pigeon's Ranch or Glorieta	March 30
14. Albuquerque	April 25
15. Peralto	April 27
Virginia	1863
16. Near Culpeper	November 5
(I, 1st Cavalry, Commanding)	
17. Stevensburg	November 8
18. Mine Run	November 26
	1864
19. Barnett's Ford	February 8
20. Near Charlottesville	March 10
21. On Rapidan River	March 11
22. Todd's Tavern	May 6
(Brevet captain) (wounded)	
23. Spotsylvania Court House	May 7
24. On the road to Beaver Dam	May 10
25. At Beaver Dam	May 10
26. On the road to Yellow Tavern	May 10
27. Yellow Tavern	May 11
28. At Meadow Bridge	May 12
29. After passing Meadow Bridge	May 13
30. Tunstall's Station	May 14
31. Tunstall's Station	May 15
32. While crossing Mattaponi River	May 27

APPENDIX

[172]

APPENDIX